"A remarkble work...It effects a much needed heroine's journey through one of the most potent and potentiating goddess archetypes...a marvelous blend of discursive and exploratory gnosis with practical and profound methodologies. Jean Houston, Ph.D, Author of *The Search for the Beloved, Godseed, Life Force, Soulcycle,* and *The Possible Human*

"It moved me...an easy style and an enjoyable selection of teaching stories" Susan Campbell, Ph.D, Author of *The Couple's Journey* and *Beyond the Power Struggle*

"Karen guides us through physical, emotional, mythical and spiritual levels of womanliness and strikes a resonant chord within us all." Carlin Diamond, M.A, author of *Love It, Don't Label It,* and Founder of Diamond W.I.S.E. World School

"The material is rich. You feel like the experience is encapsulating you." Angles Arrien, Ph.D, Cultural Anthropologist, and Author of *The Tarot Handbook*

"The complex is made simple and entertaining and you feel empowered by the experience." Donna Atkinson, M.A, Health, Education, and Psychology, and Founder of New Vistas

"I highly recommend it for woman of all ages, who are ready to move beyond old patterns and conditioning, into more fully receiving themselves in wholeness and magnificence." Darlyne Diehl, Ph.D, Hypnotherapist

"Like magic fairy dust, LaPuma sprinkles thought provoking questions throughout to gently guide you into greater self-awareness. She expands your self-image by holding a mirror for you to see your multidimensional nature, then motivates and inspires you to express these goddess qualities in your life." Gwen Sarendra, M.A, Counselor and Artist

"It's a winner! Such a timeless subject of universal interest. It's informative and helpful to anyone on the road to self-discovery." Susan Alexander, Marketing Consultant

"A comforting book, full of love...one of which a person will never tire, for there is something new in it each time you read it. Maxine Rush, Mother and Homemaker

"Great topic, breath of coverage, and concrete examples and anecodotes." Barbara Goff, Educator

**This book is dedicated to
all Goddess Warriors
and the healing of the Earth.**

A Goddess Warrior is anyone on the spiritual quest. If you believe that the Divine Light shines within, you are a Goddess.

If you are a seeker desiring to live from your Higher Self, you are a Warrior.

SoulSource Publishing

P.O.Box 877,
Fairfax, CA 94930

Awakening Female Power

The Way of The Goddess Warrior

Karen LaPuma

With Walt Runkis

Awakening Female Power,
The Way of the Goddess Warrior

Copyright, 1991 by Karen LaPuma.
SoulSource Publishing
P.O. Box 877, Fairfax, CA, 94930

Printed in the United States of America.
on Enviro-Text Recycled Acid-Free Paper

Library of Congress Catalog Card Number: 89-51331

Spiritual, Psychology, Woman's, Self-Help, New Age

Includes, List of Stories, Processes,
Metaphors and Poems
Bibliography, Glossary, Index,

ISBN: 1-878203-02-9

First Edition
10 9 8 7 6 5 4 3 2 1

Acknowledgements

My deepest appreciation and acknowledgement goes to Walter Runkis and Dorothy Tobin. If I am the "mother" of this book, then Walter is the "father," and Dorothy, the "grandmother." Many of Walter's seeds of thought have fertilized this child. Walter has also enhanced the project with creative editing. Dorothy Tobin has been a continual support with her generous editorial comments and encouragement.

Creative thought is only partly inspiration. The final product is only rearranged words and ideas plus the unique patterns which they create. My writing can be compared to a patchwork quilt. Various elements are woven together to make an original work of art.

My teachers have been many. I am deeply grateful for the psychological gifts of Carl Jung, Jean Houston, and Roberto Assagioli; for the mythological treasures of Joseph Campbell and Edith Hamilton; and for the astrological jewels of Richard Idomen, Liz Greene and Steven Arroyo. The wisdom of Buddha, Christ, Sri Ramakrishna, and Swami Satchidanada have also guided my thinking.

I truly acknowledge Angeles Arrien for her generosity, wisdom and enthusiam, and my parents, Sam and Carmella for their love and grounding influence.

I affectionately thank my friends: Lindy Ashmore, Donna Atkinson, Amy Dunn, Taeko Dickstein, M.J. Harden, LaUna Huffrines, Careayana Littman, Rose Moon, Sanaya Roman, Gwen Sarandra, Jackie Steele, and Ceclia Yarnel for their positive encouragement and support.

I want to acknowledge the Fairfax Library Reference Department, for being such a resource, Kayla and Bob Van Norman for their graphic help, Sharon Deveaux for her photographic expertise, and Irv Baker, Sue Arnold and Naomi Stenfield for their contribution to the editing.

I especially appreciate my clients and my students who have greatly contributed to this work and to my spiritual process.

Table of Contents

List of Illustrations

1. Cover by Pat Ryan
2. The Path by Karen, p.1
3. Eros Awakening Psyche by Karen, p.7
4. Goddess Warrior by Karen, p.15
5. Moon Palace by Karen, p.29
6. Goddess Warrior Logo/the Earth by Karen, p.34
7. The Well Frog by Walt, p.36
8. Mirror Metaphor by Walt, p.41
9. Mansion of the Mind by Karen, p.44
10. Who is in Charge, Anyway? by Karen, p.45
11. Earth Mandala, p.51
12. Maya by Karen, p.63
13. Integrity Symbol by Karen and Walt, p.69
14. Badge of Love and Integrity by Walt, p.71
15. The Witch and the King by Karen, p.74
16. Ragnel Transformed by Karen, p.76
17. Pearl of Great Price by Karen and Walt, p.85
18. Angel and Beast Within by Karen, p.87
19. Animal Kingdom, p.91
20. Balancing the Beast and the Higher Self by Karen, p.96
21. Tao Symbol by Walt, p.97
22. Personality Directors by Karen, p.100
23. Monkey/ Island Metaphor by Karen, p.105
24. Temple Maiden by Karen and Walt, p.113
25. Kamakala Goddess by Karen and Walt, p.115
26. Mother Earth Goddess by Karen, p.119

Preface

The Process Is the Goal

The first message I want to give you, my reader, is that if I can do it, so can you. "Do what?" you might ask. For me, it was to follow a vision that led to a quiet inner knowing, a counseling practice, and a writing career. I overcame my fear, developed faith, and gained a renewed sense of identity, self-esteem, and personal power.

I embarked upon the visionary quest because of an intense desire for purpose and to know truth. It started with a "Call to Adventure" and continues with teaching others what I need most to learn: to be my own authority, to look within, and to go beyond belief. Like the child of some mythic adventure, I was impelled to study psychology, the different metaphysical and religious systems, Eastern and Western mythologies, the physical sciences, and the practice of yoga. Through all this I learned that understanding the larger universe outside myself was just another way of reaching my personal universe within.

Awakening Female Power is a call to the woman within each of us. It is an inspirational how-to manual for anyone on the spiritual quest. Let this book be your coach--a companion to empower and heal you on your heartfelt journey to wholeness.

Your journey begins when you remember who you are. A story told by Sri Ramakrishna illustrates what I mean:

Once a pregnant tigress attacked a flock of sheep, but as she sprang upon her prey, she gave birth to a cub and died. The sheep took pity on the newborn cub and nurtured it as though it were their own. Since sheep eat grass and bleat, the cub followed their example and ate grass and bleated, too. As the cub grew into a tigress she was unaware of any differences.

One day a wild tigress came upon the herd and was amazed to see another tigress grazing with a flock of sheep. Forgetting that she was hungry, the wild tigress ran after the young tigress, seized her, and threw her to the ground. The young tigress began to bleat in terror. This was too embarrassing, so the wild tigress grabbed the youngster by the scruff of the neck and dragged her to a pool of water demanding that she look at herself. She put her face next to the young tigress and said, "Why are you eating grass? You're like me. You should be eating sheep, not bleating like them." Then the wild tigress pushed some meat into her mouth and commanded, "Eat!" The young tigress refused to swallow it, instead she began to bleat like a terrified lamb. Gradually, however, she began tasting the meat and relishing it. Then the wild tigress said, "There is no difference between you and me! Come, follow me into the forest and live the life God intended for you."

Like the wild tigress, this book is here to help you tap your true nature. The young tigress, growing up with sheep, believed she was a sheep. Similarly, we are conditioned from birth to think we are ordinary people, but we are truly Gods and Goddesses, full of divine potential. My fondest wish is to arouse your desire to seek the higher life of the soul. It is an inward turning, which demands self-discovery as its price of passage.

The soul's passage is a search for
identity and a quest for Unity.

How To Use This Book

Accept *Awakening Female Power* as an opportunity to commit to your process. It is holistic and strongly feminine, yet it draws upon the masculine. When we learn to exalt the powers of the female, and combine them with the powers of the male, a creative awakening happens.

This book will accelerate you into the experience of the Goddess by showing how to master the unproductive aspects of your nature. Reading it, and following the simple exercises, will be a rite of passage. It will compel you, first, to understand the personal myth that forms your present, and then to move beyond it into a grander vision that can become your future. Your quest for self-discovery will unfold as you read. To help you along the way there are entertaining anecdotes, drawn from ancient and modern psychological fairy tales, metaphors and myths, woven together with practical techniques, case histories, and autobiographical stories. They will encourage you to:

o   join the Great Adventure and be all you can be

o   celebrate your Divine Goddess

o   motivate your courageous Warrior

o   uncover your inner cast of characters

o   find dynamic presence

o   awaken integrity

o   develop an assertive will

o   balance your male and female

o   train the beast within

o   penetrate the unseen forces of Maya

o   maintain inner peace

o   connect with the archetypical goddesses

o   open your Goddess powers--creativity and intuition

o   nurture your own Inner Child

o   heal and forgive your past

o   raise your self-esteem

o   arouse your erotic womanly wonders

o   increase the joy of fulfillment

Use this book as a course in self-improvement. I suggest you read through it once, and then go back over it to record your insights in a journal. The key questions and processes are highlighted and indented for easy reference.

Self-searching is not only an act of self-love, it is also the first and most essential step toward altering your planet's future. As Don Quixote said, "It does not matter whether you win or lose as long as you follow the quest, and the world will be better for this."

My Personal Journey

I feel blessed that my work is helping others upon the spiritual quest, because it fills me with the inspiration and the grace of higher purpose. I feel like I am on a mission for the Goddess. *Awakening Female Power* is a distillation of my process as well as that of some of my clients, whose names were changed to protect their privacy. My partner, Walter, was a powerful resource who helped conceive this child. The path my writing took drew upon many sources, yet it maintains my own integrity.

My dreams have served as elegant tools for my understanding. The following dream came to me years ago after I had just finished my first article on the soul's journey:

I enrolled in a five-day course held on a ship that was sailing the high seas. The first three days, I studied a vast written curriculum from many sources, including myths, fairy tales, fiction, and movies. On the fourth day, I received no written material, only oral instructions, but I took copious notes. The fifth day I learned about day-to-day experience.

Upon completing the journey, everyone and everything had been transformed. Not only had us, but the ship itself was completely renovated and was now trimmed in pure gold. A special ceremony marked the ship's return. Golden stepladders streaming from the stern, carried me and a group of fellow participants. My stepladder lagged behind and was pulled to the left. I even fell into the water, but that didn't mar my appearance or enthusiasm. Upon the return, I felt as if I had been "born again." My personality had completely changed. I was no longer timid, shy, and insecure. Instead, I was full of confidence and determination.

After returning, I had to convince my teachers that my transformation was real. I had to resell them, which I did eagerly, for I knew I could do anything if I focused my energy. Feeling like a Cosmic Pied Piper, filled with inspiration and the grace of higher purpose, I began promoting the course to others. As I awoke I kept saying, "If I can do it, anyone can!"

This dream has been a guiding light, because it has become my life. As I interpret it, we are all on a spiritual quest through the University of Life. This watery earth, with its emotional storms, is our campus; our daily experiences form the curricula. My nautical adventure symbolizes my personal journey. Researching into the universal archetypes was a work that transformed me, yet I consider myself a student of life just beginning to tap the wisdom of mythology, Qabalah, and yoga.

The very essence of spiritual life is revealed through myths, symbols, metaphors, and fairy tales. What fun it has been tapping into stories as a way to understand myself. The more I learn, the more I see the connection between everything and everyone. By learning to go within to answer life's questions, I have refined my understanding of all life. The mind first clothes intuitive understanding in symbols as a means of remembering. From there, knowledge seeps into our emotional nature and finally percolates into physical reality. Only when completely absorbed can these teachings transform the personality and free the spirit from its attachment. At first, I tried to direct my intention and magically create my own reality, but ultimately I learned to let go and trust in the divine.

The stepladders represent the steps in the process. Each person has their own special way. If you are just starting, like a child, you may stumble and even skin your knee. Yet as you persist, you will began to walk, then dance through a life of balance and harmony. Being part of the process is what transforms us. Personally, I fell into emotional waters, for like most people, I needed great emotional healing. The secret was to hang on and ride out the rough spots if I wanted a joyous outcome.

My ladder streamed to the left, because originally I had an overly developed right brain. For years, I played in the astral realms of the psychic world, and I prayed for great intuitive powers. Astrology and tarot were especially rewarding, for they opened my mind to the richness of the archetypes. I believed that with these intutive powers I could serve others. Now I have found the greater wisdom of divine surrender and strive only to *be*, not to *become* .

Over the past seven years, my copious notes have grown to 900 pages. As for convincing my teachers, it was one thing to know that I wanted to write, but bringing my vision into form proved an entirely different matter. My maiden voyage was writing a book on tarot. However, six months and three drafts later, I realized that I was in over my head and "archived it." I then began a manuscript, which I called *Honoring the God/ess Within*. I abbreviated gods and goddesses to the "god/ess." This study of the archetypical subpersonalities ran three times longer than expected. Walter facetiously dubbed it *The Collected Works* , but I happily expanded it into a trilogy, entitling the first book, *A Hero's Call to Adventure*. Maybe a better title for this study would have been *The Diary of a Would-Be Hero*, for it was much too fat to fly.

Again I faced my grand dilemma. "What kind of book should I write?" I asked out loud. Almost as if in a trance, I went to a bookcase and selected Christine Downing's book, *Goddess: Mythological Images of the Feminine*. Could I have received a more magical message? Still, I didn't understand, so I asked Walter for a ritual to help begin my new undertaking. He said I would need a Latin name to depict my magical identity for my future work, so I went to the Latin dictionary, closed my eyes, opened it, and pointed directly to the word "*Virago*. " To my amazement and delight, it meant "female warrior." The magical name I chose was *Virago Via*, "the path of the female warrior." *Awakening Female Power, The Way of the Goddess Warrior* is a call to awaken. It says:

"Women, wake up your power. Everyone, wake up your consciousness and integrity. Find your center and invoke the Goddess within."

Call your Adventurer, that shining, alert self and come, follow me. Explore the journey of the Self, a visionary quest of life-long learning. The secret of a joyous, fruitful life is to trust in the process.

In all that I do, I am continually reminded that "the process is the goal."

With love and support,

Karen

Karen LaPuma

I. WAKE UP

We are the "Daughters of Time,"
Sisters of a New Day,
Born in the labor of love
And the promise of tomorrow.
We are Children of Light.
And we are here today.
We are here to stay,
The sons and the daughters of time.

Judy Collins

Introduction:

A Call to Awaken

We are all "Children of Light" and "Sisters of a New Day." New opportunities are opening to us, and we have already made a profound difference, but true equality is a prize yet to be won. Now is the time to awaken female power and heed the "Call to Adventure." Humanity desperately needs the steady, loving influence of the feminine--those immeasurable qualities that make life a dance of the divine.

Awakening Female Power calls not only women to action, but also the woman within every man. "Who are my sisters of a new day?" I once asked. I immediately found that they were men as well as women.

The Goddess Movement is truly reemerging. People everywhere are waking up to find they are all one family living on one planet. Like nature the Goddess radiates inwardly and outwardly to support all life. She lives outside, as an archetypical support; and within as loving, creative, mysterious "resources."

The Goddess Movement is a caring, spiritual, compassionate, earth-bound connection.

Psychologically the female leads us along the path to wholeness. When we awaken our female power, we listen to our bodies, feelings and intuitions, and live from the inside out. When we learn to act on our insights, we transform our lives.

Awakening the feminine is a catalyst for growth, no matter what our gender, because as the female awakens so will the male. Just as a seed needs the earth to develop, the masculine stays dormant, ever sleeping without the feminine to nurture it.

Female power is a work that is never completely finished. Unlike the quick-to-rise power of the male that slays the beast and rules over others, the erotic and enduring female ceaselessly nurtures and creates.

Female power is for all who want to awaken their inner nature and become sensitive, creative workers toward world integration. Only by owning our inner partners do we achieve integration and balance. It is a man's inner woman who bestows upon him the grace of love, and a woman's inner man who gives her the dynamic will to succeed.

Our challenge is to awaken and realize our full and whole potential, to express, not hold back. The problem is we are all asleep. Waking consciousness is just a series of discontinuous trances (little dreams we have while awake) and from these arise our beliefs about the world around us. *How do we know if our dream of the world is real? How can we learn to make the "right" decisions within the conditioned responses of our waking dream? How free are we really?*

It's Our Time

Many sources have foretold the awakening of female power. We, the sleepers, are now ready to awaken and emerge from our long night of patriarchal rule. We have lingered far too long in the twilight. It is a new decade, and again the threat of war hovers over us. The 1990's are being heralded as a time of great collective change. Only global healing can realign and balance the delicate web of life. Effort to save our earth is already in motion. Presently, we are caught in transition. We are experiencing the death throes of the old cycle--the darkness before the light of a new human understanding. The complexities of modern society, and an ever-increasing corruption and disillusionment in business, religion, and government have created a crisis of purpose. As Anais Nin said, "the risk of remaining closed in the bud is more painful than the risk it takes to blossom."

The changes are happening deep inside us. The time is ripe. Hindus and Buddhists believe we are entering the Kali Yuga, or the age of Kali, the Great Goddess. Kali is the Warrior Goddess who embodies Transformation and the Power of Time--the primordial principle of evolution. She closes the old era by giving birth to the new; creating and consuming in ever-changing cycles. The Goddess will restore the divine female nature that we have lost.

The resurgence of the Divine Female is upon us. At long last, it is the Age of Woman.

Jean Houston in *The Search for the Beloved*, commented on the timeliness of awakening the genius of the female. This awakening is critical to human survival. "Women are at long last joining, as full partners, in the business of human affairs." Women have expanded their horizons by entering into every field of human endeavor after having reached a near-saturation point in their pre-occupation with child rearing. After centuries of gestation in the womb of preparatory time, the awakening of female power is achievable. Vital to this effort is the emergence of the disciplined female mind. The dawn of the dynamic feminine is perhaps the most important event in recorded history. Its effects will surely create unimaginable change in our cultural evolution.

John Naisbitt and Patricia Aburdene's *Megatrends 2000, Ten Directions for the 1990's* called the 1990's the decade of women in leadership. The dominant shift in business is from "management" to "leadership" or from centrally controlling an enterprise to fostering the best in those people who are performing the work. They said that in the last two decades two thirds of the new jobs created in the information era were given to women. This trend is expected to continue into the next millennium.

Astrologers say we are witnessing the dawn of the Aquarian Age. It is a New Age.

The New Age is not a time or place but an expanded state of consciousness.

Regardless of our apparent failures, there is a profound promise that humanity will grasp this vision of universal wholeness and interconnectedness with all nature. Alice A. Bailey, who wrote 24 volumes on metaphysics, called this New Age the "Age of Synthesis," where the female would come into her full power. The New Age will unfold by restoring the Golden Balance between the feminine and masculine principles.

Terry Cole-Whittaker, in *Love and Power in a World Without Limits* welcomes this Golden Age by saying, "We must dare again or die." Our only salvation as women and the only hope to save our children and restore our precious Earth is to cast off our cloak of unconscious forgetfulness and remember who we are. "The full awakening of the female will create a cosmic event heretofore unexperienced."

To fully take part in the Divine Dance of Creation, cultivate the motivation and purpose needed to throw open the doors to life's great bounty. Active participation comes to us when we finally believe in ourselves and find the guts to follow our hearts upon the Grand Adventure.

The Journey of the Soul

The call to awaken means to act from the light of the soul. The soul is our essence, our individualized spirit that remains eternally linked with Divine Consciousness. The soul prevails beyond time and space. It existed before the life of our bodies and holds the accumulated knowledge of all our past lives. Knowing no limits, the soul always knows best. To listen to our soul's messages, we need to look for its signs indirectly through our inner nature--the Goddess. The soul uses daily situations, which are sometimes hardships, to strengthen and develop those qualities needed for spiritual evolution.

The Great Myths are the world's dreams. These cosmic designs are our soul's stories, which form invisible templates that support our transformations. The secret of joyful living is encoded within these time-honored tales. A myth allows us the experience of oneness by invoking images that reflect our inner struggles. In the course of writing this book, I "became" each mythic character and lived each universal pattern deeply. I immersed myself in the soul's many faces and intimately experienced my mystical heredity and multi-dimensional nature.

Universal principles are like computer programs; they must be stored in memory before they can yield a result. As you read through this book, you will have an affinity for certain stories, myths, and metaphors. Remember these tales! They will reveal issues that have special meaning for you and will serve as metaphors for your deepest psychic feelings.

During this psychological journey it is helpful to look upon the personality as an androgynous being, derived from a constellation of different patterns. Carl Jung termed these "archetypes." I called them "god/ess." Myths, archetypes, and god/ess chronicle the ageless wonders of the psyche. They are thumb-prints of who we are. As we open to symbology, we merge our personal life with the universal.

Joseph Campbell explored many different mythological motifs and found that one grand pattern emerged that was the mother of them all. This great allegory is the visionary quest known as the Hero's Journey. Also called "soulmaking," it begins when the seeker first questions, and ends only when the soul passes from darkness into light. This sacred psychology is the heart and foundation of the Great Work, described by alchemists as "transmuting the lead of ego into the pure gold of the Higher Self."

To become in actuality what we are in essence is the heart of the soulmaking. Answering the quest always calls for a higher life. There are risks, unknowns to face, and attachments to discard, but this Adventure prepares us for the greater life of the soul.

Soulmaking offers a chance to stop marching to the beat of instinctual behavior patterns and dance within a symphony of free thinking.

It is a woman finding herself by breaking free of her worn-out roles. It is a man reclaiming his intuitive feelings and winning through compassion and cooperation. It is overcoming an obsession with material possessions and trading in false security for love and independence. It is a mother balancing her many duties and still having time for herself. Soulmaking is making it in the world with your creative wits and doing the only work worth doing, working toward the greater good of the whole.

The essence of the Hero's Journey is to venture forth into the realm of the supernatural; encounter awesome forces; learn to act decisively; conquer the evil within; rid the land of ignorance; and return victorious to release new life into the world. We learn to explore the realm of God through a process of separation, initiation and return.

Finding New Models

We can expand self-knowledge by embodying a new personal myth that shines beyond the traditional male/female role. Let the Goddess Warrior light the way to global interconnectedness. This model shows us how to heal ourselves, and in so doing, heal the Earth. The Goddess tells us to celebrate our divinity, trust, be creative, and open our compassionate hearts.

The Warrior urges us to be strong and courageous, to combat our sheep-like conditioning, and dispel our inner darkness. This inner Warrior is our soul's Motivator--the spirit of adventure that ignites our urge to embark upon the visionary quest. The Warrior is our Prime Mover, who prods us into action by choosing to be present. Being a Warrior means participating in our own process with awareness in every moment. It means deciding, just for the joy of it, to do battle with the forces of ignorance and injustice. It means mounting our steed of higher purpose and charging off into the rising sun of self-knowledge, balance, and Unity.

As Goddess Warriors, we become living images of divinity and strength, faith and courage, a blend of female and male united. Heed the Goddess Warrior's call:

"WAKE UP
BE CENTERED and
INVOKE THE GODDESS."

**Mount your Steed of Higher Purpose
Identify with the Goddess Warrior**

Judy Collins' song, "Daughters of Time," has been a guiding inspiration for me. Her words urge us to be strong and have the courage to try, for it is our time and "we are no longer alone." She tells us that we can find peace in a new world, by moving away from the past and being the best that we can be.

The image of Kali (see Chapter 11) tells us to cut away our old selves, to release outmoded beliefs and relationships, to dispel fear, enhance spirit, express ourselves, seek discrimination and knowledge, and let go attachments. Her mission is to annihilate all that obstructs the truth. Her fight is the eternal battle between knowledge and ignorance, truth and falsehood, oppressor and oppressed.

Theologian, Matthew Fox, called Hildegard of Bingen (the enlightened prophet, artist, and scientist who lived 800 years ago) "the ideal model of the liberated woman." Hildegard foretold that the spirit of woman would bring about God's work, and her influence is all the more significant in view of the patriarchal nature of her period. She was the first woman to write to women. Hildegard's teachings urged women to wake up, embrace wisdom, establish social justice, and celebrate their holiness. The message is still potent for us today.

Who are your models? Are they Super Mom, Wonder Woman, the political and enterprising Jane Fonda, the feminist Gloria Steinem, the tragic Marilyn Monroe, the innovative Cher?

It is interesting how the Madonna/Whore complex of the past has merged in the teen idol Madonna. This provocatively sexual rebel is an ambitious, brassy blond, who has become a metaphorical finger in the face of the status quo. What she's got, a great many people want. Her main ingredients for popularity are sexual energy and a willingness to break outmoded taboos and boundaries. She is a wounded child, whose songs urge us to express and respect ourselves and stand up to patriarchy and racism. As the "Material Girl," she embodies the modern image of an archetypical Maiden of Desire.

Today's kids have She-Ra, Princess of Power--an erotic female warrior who daily fights the forces of evil. All we had was Minnie Mouse, Olive Oyle, Lucy, and Gracie. It's a wonder we survived it.

It is advantageous to personally identify with positive images and role models, for we all need an appropriate context in which to live our personal vision. It is up to us to make new heroic figures, and dig up the old ones. Merlin Stone's *Ancient Mirrors of Womanhood,* offers *A Treasury of Goddess and Heroine Lore from Around the World* from which to choose.

Before you create new models, examine your personal motivation. What is your style? Do you mainly focus on pleasing and caring for others? Does your lust for pleasure drag you down the path of life? Do security based fears plague you? Do you let higher goals inspire you to grow to be the best that you can be?

The Call to Adventure

Before beginning the adventure of soulmaking, you must ask yourself if you are truly committed to self-discovery and self-improvement. *Are you willing to accept the challenge? Are you ready to participate fully in life in the highest and best way possible?*

If you answer the Call, you are a Warrior, but you only become a Hero if you are willing to ceaselessly combat the dark forces that you carry within yourself. To encourage your soul's purpose, arm yourself with integrity, focus, practice and nonattachment and your Goddess powers will awaken naturally. It is through our daily process that we answer the Call.

We are told supernatural aids will come to help, heralds will appear, and doors will magically open. You do not have to rely solely upon your own innate powers. Christ said, "I can of mine own self do nothing." Support comes directly from within or through a vast array of "outside sources." All you have to do is ask, and a sign from the universe will show you an appropriate way.

You will need commitment to follow the quest, awaken your Divine nature, and then return to use that vision for the good of all. A Goddess Warrior soon learns that all natural order exists as a process of perpetual rise and fall.

To understand this process, plant a seed, watch it sprout, grow to blossom, put forth seed and return to root. Meister Eckhart said, "The seed of God is in us. . .it will thrive and grow up to God." In nature, growth begins only after the seed is buried in darkness. Our wounds allow the essence of our immortality to sprout. Our adversities become the fertile ground in which our roots grow. We propagate our spiritual seed by living with integrity and by trusting our connection with our Source. Purpose waters the sprout. But, it may take years to know if the seeds we plant will flower into roses or gardenias. Tending the garden is the primary aim of our life. If we trust our natural timing, and prune when appropriate, our ideals will sprout and grow to fill our hearts. Our identities will evolve and branch out into the world around us.

If you are reluctant to follow your vision and if you close your mind to the quest, you not only miss the greatest adventure of all time, but you are in danger of becoming another "victim who needs to be saved." Life without purpose always seems futile, even if you have worldly fortune. Campbell says that it is like climbing a ladder, only to find that when you reach the top, you are on the wrong side of the house.

A special summons goes to those of you who do not yet know that you are seeking the higher life. If you feel as if there is something missing, if you lack that special magic, or if you feel as if you are standing still while running in the "rat race" as fast as you can, welcome aboard. Awaken your female power and merge your destiny within the Great Destiny by choosing to be a Goddess Warrior.

Humankind alone is called to co-create.

Hildegard

1

Choosing the Goddess Warrior

Do you know you have the ability to create a new life? Power is accepting responsibility for creating your own situations and knowing that you have the knowledge and insight to transmute each experience into wisdom.

Our greatest power is choice. We have a right to choose, and without manipulating, create what we want. We have the power to say what is important in our lives. We always have choices, but do we really accept ourselves enough to choose? Ask yourself, *"What do I have to do to take conscious charge of my life and follow the light of my soul?"* Choose consciously what adds love and value to your life, what supports your aliveness, and what nurtures you. Choose, by rallying your soul's Guardian: that part dedicated to being your own person. Goethe said, "Whatever you can do or dream you can, begin it. Boldness has genius, power and magic in it."

Our true nature is powerful, creative, and loving. We exist independent of the opinions of others. Whether we are aware of it or not, we weave our own universe from the thoughts we think, the decisions we make, the actions we take, and the beliefs and expectations we have.

Our purpose is to make the contribution we want to make. Our deepest satisfaction comes from contributing to others and doing something about our life.

Honoring the Virgin Goddess

The first thing to do is rejoice in your own shining individuality and believe in yourself. A positive self-regard is essential. You are a Divine Child, so trust yourself and become a living star in your own eyes. "To thine own self be true" was the message of Hamlet. Recognize your personal worth by honoring your own uniqueness and expressing yourself through writing.

Give yourself plenty of time to answer the following questions in your journal: What are my strengths? What makes me distinct from others? What are my natural abilities and talents, those things I enjoy doing? What are my weaknesses? How can I compensate for these failings? What are those things that are not working in my life? Do I freely choose to do what I want to do and say or do I spend my time pleasing and placating others? Examine all of your activities on a typical day, then ask yourself, do I like this and/or that?

Awaken your Virgin Goddess by learning to focus your attention on what matters to you. Untouched by others, this separate self needs no one to experience a sense of completeness. Hear the Virgin's voice that says, "I've got to be me." "I've got to do my thing." "I have virtue and integrity and I will not compromise what I know." She is your pure essence.

You live from her when you learn to say, "No" to what you don't want and, "Yes" to what you do want. Do not put your dreams aside to help others with theirs or dissipate your creative force in relationships, so that nothing is left for you. Promise yourself to do what is right for you, not just what others may want you to do, or what you think you should do out of a sense of obligation. Otherwise, you get lost in the less productive currents of the life force and unconsciously slip into roles that others create for you. One client said she was 22 before she first asked, "When will I have my own opinion, instead of just parroting the words and thoughts of others?"

You empower your Virgin by going within, seeking knowledge, and joining with others of like-mind. (More on the archetypal Virgin goddesses in Chapters 11, 12 and 14.)

Overcoming the Obstacles

Awakening female power means acting from the light of the soul. Like the little tigress, our soul's light is often covered with a blanket of tradition. As we prepare for power, we must also prepare for contest.

For millennia, women have been conditioned to seek approval, to submit, and to subordinate themselves to their male peers. Tradition encouraged women to project their creative energy onto their men instead of wielding it themselves. Women were to keep their creativity within the family circle and out of the "real world." This pattern has changed dramatically, but as Congresswoman Patricia Schoeder recently called to our attention by quoting a United Nations report: "Women of the world still provide two thirds of all the hours worked upon the planet, receive but 10 percent of the wages, and control only 1 percent of the property."

Deeply ingrained social attitudes in both men and women have created unconscious behavior patterns that subtly and continuously devalue the role of women. It comes in dozens of ways, but the message is always the same: "You're just not as good." This attitude is a serious handicap. Many of us have fallen victim to this notion and continually limit ourselves. We believe what we were told, and do what others want us to do. We put the needs of everyone else first.

Our mothers and grandmothers perpetuated these beliefs. Once I made a big issue about how, when my mother would visit, she would change and wash my brother's bed sheets, but not mine. Mothers program their daughters by the way they train their sons.

There are real and imagined barriers that keep us from awakening our power and going for what we want. *What are the barriers that keep you from achieving your goals?* If you're not living in joy and don't have what you want, it should be obvious you are struggling with limiting beliefs.

Probing Your Belief Systems

Question your beliefs, what you were told, your values, and your lifestyle. Search yourself to see if you operate within a limiting cage of sabotage. Do voices from the past cloud your vision? Did someone tell you, "it's a man's world and you are second best"? Beliefs like, "I'm not enough," or "others are better," imprison us behind the bars of our self-imposed limitations.

Since our experiences reflect our beliefs, any limiting beliefs will be mirrored in our relationships and/or our bodies. We create illnesses and attract people who show us what we resist in ourselves. People do to us what we do to ourselves. Our ability to choose becomes ensnared in these veils of learned behavior patterns. Yet, we can change our beliefs and learn new ones.

In my past I had some painful lessons concerning a compulsive urge to serve others. I alternated feeling my place was either "to help fix things" or "subordinate myself." The beliefs behind these behaviors were: "To be loved, I must submit and please" or "If I express my dynamic powerful self, I'll lose love." These are oppressive thoughts for anyone! My new aphorism is, "As my power increases, so does my joy and love in my relationships." The truth is that all people are divine and whole, having both a feminine and masculine nature. It's great to be loving and compassionate, and also intelligent and dynamic.

Where we put our attention determines the nature of the experiences we draw to us. The amount of attention we give something is equal to the amount of feeling behind it. If there is fear present, it becomes an especially powerful web that ensnares us in survival, avoidance, and struggle. Our freedom comes by penetrating beliefs. Describe a belief and clear any strong emotions concerning it, and it loses its power.

Observe your limiting beliefs. Define it. What is the pattern? What did your family and your culture tell you? Are there conflicting voices within you? How does it restrict you? What is its pain? Experience it. How does it feel? What is its texture? What does it keep saying to you? Placing attention on it gives you the opportunity to let it go. Relinquish the pain. Grieve it and make space for your healing.

Understanding Emotional Bonding

Women's programming is reinforced by their emotional make-up. Women are often uncomfortable when asserting themselves, even if they are in a position of authority. Carol Gilligan's *In A Different Voice* explains why. She finds that men tend to fantasize about what they will do to someone, whereas women fantasize about what will be done to them. The problem begins in infancy: A baby girl fixes her identity while still bonded to her mother, but a baby boy must grow up and separate from his mother in order to fix his identity with his father. This variation in bonding patterns is the principal reason women seek closeness and dependency through relationships, while men tend to seek separateness and autonomy. Whether we are aware of it or not, these basic tendencies color everyone's behavior.

We break these bonding patterns by accepting responsibility for ourselves in each moment, by listening to our bodies, our feelings, our intuition, and our thoughts.

Lilly's Story

Lilly and Todd's relationship mirrors this bonding dichotomy. When Todd talked about his relationship with Lilly, it was clear that they had a telepathic agreement between them. Lilly, like many women, learned to win her mate's approval by supporting him and relinquishing her own powers of choice. Todd had first thought this quite natural. In Todd's words, "Girls always agree to be 'second banana,' because they know men can turn ape and beat up on them." Being "top banana" appealed to Todd, at least for a while. He said, "I liked having someone around who always let me have things my own way."

Unfortunately, neither knew how debilitating this arrangement would become for Lilly. Over the years Lilly grew more passive, subservient, and helpless. Todd was disgusted with her simpering, but he had to admit, that step by step, he had trained her for the role by not letting her express her feelings. She feared his intimidation and stopped acting from her own authority. She tried hard not to do anything that would upset him. She was afraid, that if she asserted her own will, she would be "frozen out," unloved and unwanted. This imbalance of power destroyed all hope of their ever finding happiness. Eventually, they separated.

Lilly then was able to quickly find joy in her independent Virgin self. Shortly after separating from Todd, her mother died, and her only daughter went off to college. She now faced only one relationship: the one with herself. She opened her mind and worked on her process, which included exercise, meditation and therapy. She found joyful peace in having her own little home and her support system.

Lilly said, "I surrendered to a higher power, for I knew I couldn't do it alone. I started taking care of myself, instead of always taking care of others." Lilly stopped looking for gratification outside herself, and found it waiting patiently within. She became mindfully conscious and realized, she was an interesting and enjoyable companion. After she found herself, she went on to find a loving and dynamic relationship with a year-long friend who became her lover.

Life challenges are designed to build our strength. *What are the obstacles that deprive you of power?* Whatever the blockages, we can release them by reclaiming the potential within us. We must look upon our obstacles, not as insufferable plagues, but as opportunities for growth. Sometimes we can avoid obstacles, but when we cannot, it is a time of learning, and we must not look away.

Moving Beyond the Past

In the past, women lived out the old Lunar/Venusian myth by being categorized as either Madonnas or Whores. They were either stuffed into the mother role or looked upon as sex toys. Awakening the many faces of the Goddess is a sure way to go beyond these worn out female roles.

Men have enjoyed a more solar existence. They are shored up by the myth of a strong, war-like Mars. The Old Male archetype is competitive and out for himself. His way is to control and overpower, but statistically he dies sooner. He "lives" in his head and gonads, denying anyone, including himself, access to his feelings and dependencies. He allows anger, but all other emotions are considered a weakness.

Such men, especially, need support during this time of transition. They experience pain if they do and pain if they don't. If they act from their feminine nature, they may suffer social and perhaps economic loss; however, if they do not, they suffer physical and emotional damage.

The Feminist Movement stimulated women's fight for equal rights. Angeles Arrien said it should have been called the "Anima Movement," for many of these women were like a woman within a man. In the push to be strong, independent thinkers, many women found power and transcended the old stigmas, only to become like the Old Male. This life-sustaining movement of the past is merging into the life-generating Goddess Movement, as we learn to temper our power with love.

One of my clients, an aging Jewish Mother, inherited her husband's art gallery when he suddenly died. She felt very insecure, for the only preparation she received was the advice her husband gave her on his deathbed: "Run the business the same way you run the family. Don't try to be a man. Just do it the way you always do it." That is what she did and it worked wonderfully. She had to make sure that "cash in" balanced "cash out," but more profoundly she treated her employees as part of her family and they served her like they would serve their own mothers. Female power is the power of caring. It is about opening our hearts and loving--realizing we are one family and yet complete within ourselves.

How do we, armed only with our female power, fight a society dominated by the Old Male? How can we face these patriarchal fathers and change the face of society? Jesus said, "The meek shall inherit the earth." Young David wrote poetry, sang and danced before God, but went on to face Goliath and win. It was a frail poet who turned the tide of war, not the mighty masculine horde of Israel. Although our task seems overwhelming, it is not, if we start with ourselves and carry balance into every activity and every relationship. This means focusing inside and acting on what comes from within through our words and actions. Despite our intense programming, if we trust in ourselves, we can embrace adversity with a sense of curiosity and adventure. And if we have a winning mindset, we'll win. The principal benefit of each conquest is always greater understanding.

Jo's Story

Jo suffers from agoraphobia (a morbid fear of open or public places) and wrote to me about her feelings of helplessness. She said her life was VERY restricted and controlled. She described it as a "living hell." Early in life, Jo was conditioned to be ruled by fear and to take care of everyone else at her own expense. Over the years her lifestyle slowly sucked her into this devastating disease. She had scarcely left her home in over fifteen years. She rarely even went shopping. Finally, at 53, she began to question authority, saying, "It was only recently that I ever even thought about what might happen if I did this or that. Before it was just that some great-unknown-horrible-thing will happen if I do such and such."

At 18 Jo married to get away from a cold and bitter home life; only to find herself under the rule of an authoritarian husband. He refused to let her work or have friends over and demanded she serve his every whim. She said, "It was easier to give in and do what he wanted than to suffer the consequences. He never raised a hand to me, but the psychological beatings are indescribable." She didn't know she had a choice and thought that pleasing others was the only way to get personal recognition and some feeling of self-importance. Now she realizes, "This is wrong. A person cannot ever find happiness through other people. You have to be happy with yourself first." She added, "I used to think having people care for me was the most important thing in the world, but now I know that it is more important to have respect for myself. If you're dependent on the responses of others, you are always at someone else's mercy, but if you set your own standards, you have control over your own life."

Jo's comment, "Every time a person gives in, they give up their views, and eventually they lose a part of themselves," is painfully true. We cheat ourselves as well as others by allowing them to program our decisions, opinions, and choices. In essence, we become less whole.

For Jo, breaking her patterns was a painful practice, but she is breaking them and is now healing. Jo learned she had the choice to say no to someone's request when it was not what she wanted to do. She said no to getting up at five in the morning to make her husband breakfast. That was a big step, but saying no to a local bully and taking him to court was a major step.

For years Jo had been harassed by an alcoholic neighbor, an Old Male type, who frequently went out of his way to make her isolation even more unbearable. After his latest drunken threats and despite her phobia and her desire for peace, she had him arrested and appeared in court to testify. Jo was exhibiting bravery, because she was much afraid, but did it anyway. Confidence comes by taking action. She said, "It isn't so much the winning or losing that's important, but just taking the bull by the horns for a change and attacking an issue, instead of running from it."

Her hardships have pushed her back into life and provided the opportunities for her to bring forth the person she is inside. She realized she must love this bully for being a catalyst for her new-found strength. She also saw how his behavior was a part of his conditioning and she pitied him. Still, justice must prevail and she made her protest by taking a stand against his obtrusive behavior and won.

She learned that by just choosing--little choices made in the moment--she could calm her fearful phobic Inner Child with her powerful wise inner woman and act with composure and confidence. Her willingness to take action and follow her feelings, even though it was a stretch, proved empowering. Now, she can stand up to authority figures, and is even able to go into crowded public places by herself.

Beware of the "Moon Palace"

If we do not make choices for ourselves, we do not own our light. We become a suspended floating offspring--a resident of the "Moon Palace." Poet and author Robert Bly tells an Eskimo fairy tale:

Many women become stranded, a long way from Earth, in a place called the Moon Palace. It is a realm where we see only by reflected light; the light of others, not our own. Women go there when they feel separated from life and not citizens of the Great Existence. They get there by not taking responsibility for their own growth.

This story says to take hold of the rope, and with your eyes closed, slide down. However, before your feet touch the Earth, you must open your eyes and jump, otherwise you will become a spider entrenched in a web.

This tale stresses the importance of opening your eyes and jumping before you land. It is important that you choose to wake up. Those who refuse, bind themselves within a world of their own denial. They would rather live unconsciously than actively participate in life--they lose touch with their feet and turn into spiders. They live a life of endless tragedy, bound within their own webs, which they spin from an inexhaustible supply of complaints and intrigue.

Bly believes that as many as half the women in the U.S. are semi-permanent residents of the Moon Palace. Many women live there for years. Some are married and yet feel tremendous loneliness. They may be surrounded by babies, families, and friends, yet they are still uninterested in life. This separateness is a major issue that has not yet been adequately addressed by the Feminist Movement.

If you feel disconnected, as if you're suspended a long way from Earth, actually you are not that far away. All you have to do is take hold of the rope--the invisible Goddess force within-- and slide down.

Discover your Wise One within, (see Chapeter12) and be escorted through the crossroads of life. Trust that you will find your line to freedom and those answers you seek.

Embrace your Goddess connection and begin relating to your world from the inside out. Know there is support--just ask. Go inside to your beautiful fertile valley and your deep inner pond. Let the Goddess guide you to your inner source of joyful creativity.

Getting Grounded

To break free of the inertia and irresponsibility of the Moon Palace, you must call upon the aid of your Warrior

If you feel disconnected, as if you are a
long way from Earth, actually you aren't.
Take hold of the rope--the invisible
Goddess Force within--and slide down.

and get grounded. Grounded is a term that means you are connected to your body, your environment and to your own truth.

Lora, a dynamic corporate executive who makes over a hundred thousand dollars a year said, "The secret of my power is being grounded." Before Lora learned the benefits of "presence," she was flighty. She would not always pay attention to what was going on; her mind would day-dream and drift away. Consequently she did not always know what she felt, nor could she act from her true center. Lora said, "I would slip out of my body into fantasy, because it was often too painful to stay with what I was really feeling. But, escaping out of the body proved to be a temporary relief at best. This means of solving my problems often made me sick because I could not read my body's messages." Lora then added, "Being grounded is a real choice for health."

Just by choosing to concentrate in the moment and doing a daily grounding ritual, she is alert and present. Lora is now being taken seriously. She said, "Not only have I been seen in the business world, but more importantly, being grounded has connected me with my own creativity. Only by being present has spontaneous right action been allowed to take place." Remember, grounding means deciding to stay focused in the moment and doing a daily ritual such as the following active imagery:

Breathe in and breathe out deeply and rhythmically. Soften your body; soften your mind. Imagine there is a cord coming from the base of your spine, going down deep into the earth. Connect the cord to the center of the earth. Breathe the reddish brown earth energy into your feet. Then bring the cord back from the center of the earth through your body, threading along the spine, passing your stomach, your throat, your head, and out into the ceiling and sky. Now, imagine that cord is a funnel and open your head. Bring in the light of the cosmic sun. Feel your head being flooded with celestial rays. Now, feel your feet on the ground and your head in the heavens, but focus your energy into your center, wherever you may sense it to be. Breathe into your center. Say I am one with my body, my environment and my truth. I am one with the Goddess.

Harness your personal energy by expressing yourself a little at a time. One step at a time is how you become the master of your own life. You can break your conditioning and release your natural resistance by knowing that you have choices--little choices in the moment. You stay out of the Moon Palace when you learn to be courageously patient, dare to follow your personal vision, and are persistent at "keeping on." We can break those past patterns by identifying with the Goddess Warrior.

Embodying the Goddess Warrior

A Goddess Warrior's purpose is to live , love and co-create in harmony with the Great Goddess.

Co-creation means asking for what we want, but being receptive and surrendering to a Higher Will. Each of us is an unique expression of the Divine. Let us all create with love, moving beyond our little personal world and work to save the Earth. "No easy task," you may say. Indeed it's true, but not for the reason you may think. To transform humanity, you first transform yourself. Change yourself and the rest takes care of itself.

Being a Goddess means trusting in the divine connection. It is knowing that we are blessed with light and creative resources. It means adopting an attitude of receptivity, acceptance and appreciation. The world of the Goddess is one of abundance and attraction. It comes alive when we choose to act from our inner impulses, for only then are we in harmony with the universe.

A positive attitude is everything. Don't allow yourself to wallow in emotional swamp lands. Watch that you don't hold your feelings back. Instead, find ways to express emotions without dumping them onto others. Take care of yourself and be around people who make you feel alive.

Being a Warrior means choosing and re-choosing to participate in your own processes with gentleness and awareness in every moment. It means Being-Here-Now! The word "warrior" implies compassionate leadership and a strategy of presence. If you choose the Goddess Warrior's path, you will need a strategy or plan of action that operates within the Tao--the Will of the Goddess.

Setting and Reaching Goals

What do you want to get out of life? Can you define your personal goals? Without setting goals, you remain limited. With goals you strengthen your power and your control over your life. It is easy, once you learn to focus on the changes you want to make and stay in the present while achieving them. You need to observe your limitations and then take action toward overcoming those restrictions. James Fadiman in his book, *Unlimit Your Life, Setting and Getting Goals*, said, "If you know where you want to go and are determined to get there, nothing can prevent you, once you are willing to start, willing to continue, and willing to deserve the rewards." *Are you willing to allow yourself to have your choices?*

Success is only a state of mind. Our power to succeed is directly linked to our self-confidence. In the final analysis, it is who we believe we are that most affects our performance in the world. Be aware, however, that moving beyond what is comfortable and familiar may create an identity crisis, causing an unconscious slow down. Radical changes in lifestyle may affect how safe we feel. We may even become sick as we begin to experience this change toward success and power. The important key is: Don't stop! When you don't allow yourself to quit or turn back, you will ultimately be successful at whatever you attempt to do. Remember that Edison had thousands of failures before finding the right filament to make a light bulb.

It is time to bring our dreams out into the world and co-create with the Divine. Dare to manifest your soul's power. Know it is safe and necessary. As you open to believing in yourself and your ability to co-create with the Divine, you allow our heart's desires to come to you. Choose what you want and then be unattached to the outcome. Go the Way of the Goddess Warrior. Everyone who does ultimately wins.

Memorize the following Goddess Warrior's affirmation to identify with your soul's Guardian.

I am a Goddess Warrior,
A mixture of divinity and strength.
I am faith and courage.
I am being and doing.
I am Love and Will.

I am the Great Adventurer,
Feminine and masculine, shining in One.
Integration is my goal,
Creation, my pleasure, and
A centered self, my mode of play.

Motivated to express my inner creativity,
And follow my heart's desire,
I move with purpose and surrender,
To actualize my individuality,
Within the circle of humanity.

Let me do my work in the world.
Let the illumination of my heart be
Divine Love serving Divine Will...
Let wholeness and enlightenment
Be my way.

Living behind a shield of love and integrity,
Spontaneously in the present,
Doing perfect actions,
I conquer and forgive my adversaries, and
Become a Living Light.

> *Soulmaking requires that we die to one story and be reborn to a larger one.*
>
> Jean Houston

2

Seeing Beyond the Present Myth

The greatest challenge faced by all Goddess Warriors is to release the past and follow their grandest vision into the future. The question is, ***"Is your grandest vision grand enough?"***

Awakening female power is learning to see beyond your range of present possibilities. A tale told by Sri Ramakrishna about a frog who lived in a well will explain what I mean:

> Once upon a time there was a frog who lived happily within the shelter of a deep well. Her home was safe and comfortable. She had been born there and, as far back as she could remember, she had always lived there. She knew all there was to know about her well and was only too happy to tell anyone who came for water.
>
> One day the well frog saw a sailor fetching water. When he lowered his jug into the well, something jumped out and landed with a loud splash. The little well frog could hardly believe her eyes, for there climbing up onto her rock was another frog.
>
> "Where did you come from?" asked the well frog.
>
> "I came from the ocean--it's a very big place."
>
> "Really, how big? Is it this big?" the well frog asked, as she leaped to a rock halfway across the well.

"Much larger--I mean it's enormous," was the ocean frog's reply.

Preposterous, thought the well frog. She puffed herself up, marshaled all her strength, and made a mighty leap from one side, completely across the well, to a rock on the other side, proudly proclaiming, "Well, it can't possibly be any larger than this."

To some extent we are all like well frogs, living within the safe confines of our limited mental, emotional, and perceptual structures.

Can't be bigger than this!

Exploring Your Personal Myth

Everyone's life is a myth. Your personal myth is formed out of everything you do. It is a snapshot of your individual human development. Coded within your personal myth are layers upon layers of personality programming, universes existing within universes. Each person's mythical reality is different. Finding the elements of your personal myth is what propels your spirit forward and sustains you in this world. Your personal myth defines the scope of your evolutionary journey, yet it also serves as a perimeter defense system, insulating you from the experience of the outside world. As the quest for identity unravels like a personal yarn, it leads you along a winding trail, through the grand pageant of your personal stories, interests, values, and dreams. Finally you gaze within the mystery of your own immortal soul.

Observe yourself with your friends and with others. What are your stories? What are those anecdotes that you love to tell? Your stories are alive, dynamic, and full of emotional imagination. They form the structure of your "well frog," your memories and beliefs. They are what you exchange with others, which are in part, directly related to who is listening. You tell different stories to your doctor than you might tell to an acquaintance at a party. It does not matter who is listening, your stories are reevaluated and enlivened every time you tell them. Your personal myth forms an unconscious bridge between you and your listener that transcends factual truth. You must discover your stories, not to change them, but to enrich and expand them in order to release the latent power within them.

Examining the Childhood Messages

You can begin to understand your personal myth by examining your favorite mythological stories, fairy tales, and legends. *Become your Inner Child. Which childhood fables and fairy tales come to mind?* These treasured allegories appealed to you as a child because each offered food for your emerging soul. Immerse yourself in their special feeling and find their messages buried deep within your memories. You may discover that the entire cast of characters is all alive and well and still working for

your well-being, just as it has since you were a child.
Some are the unlikeliest heroes.

I grew up watching Popeye on television. My cousins
even called me "Olive Oyle" when I was a budding maiden. I resented the nickname but as I look back, I realize
I <u>was</u> like Olive Oyle--lanky, gullible, naive, and very
female.

Popeye is an excellent example of a modern myth. He
was a mild-mannered warrior who constantly fought the
forces of evil, represented by his arch foes, Bluto and the
Sea Hag. To me Bluto and the Sea Hag represent the
outer world of brute patriarchal force and our inner
depths of magical, dreamy, emotional self. Popeye tried
everything to avoid conflict but could never pass up an
opportunity to defend the rights of the weak and innocent. He would go to great lengths not to get angry and
always took a severe stomping before calling upon his supernatural strength, which he invoked by eating spinach.

Eating spinach is doing what we may not want to do,
but doing it anyway, because it is good for us. Spinach
also embodies the "greening power," or the natural, abundant, creative force of feminine divinity (the catalyst that
transforms all adversity).

Popeye had only one eye, which brings to mind the
biblical passage where Christ says, "When the eye is one,
the life is full of light." There is also Popeye's famous saying, "I am's what I am's and that's all what I am's," which
is a spiritual message similar to that received by Moses.
God's reply, when Moses asked for His name, was "I Am
That I Am." Popeye was a true hero who taught me and
millions of other children the lessons of duty, ethical perfection, and healthy living.

Defining Your Sacred Wounds

Every personal myth has a sacred wound to heal. It is
part of our mystical heritage. *Define your wounds, your
special pains, for they reveal the larger story.* Your
wounds could be an insecurity, a sensitivity, a personality
trait, a past relationship, the death of a loved one, or the
end of a love affair. My wound was emotional neediness,
which was a constant source of pain. Yet through this
sacred wound I opened my love nature and found my cal-

ling. Houston says, "Wounding is an invitation to our renaissance. The wound is the critical act through which the mortal achieves divinity."

Don't be afraid to experience your pain, for it is the seed from which your greater expansion grows. Let your pain lead you inward to discover the Divine. Any pain can be magically transmuted into a sacred wound if used as a tool for personal growth. By allowing your pathos to penetrate to the core of your being, you are finally healed.

A wound is often the magical ingredient that pushes us beyond the ramparts of the old obsolete stories that deny our full humanity. The wound is an indication that the old form is ready to die, despite the reluctance of the personality, and a sign that our personal myth is beginning to flower.

Answering, Who Am I?

When we search our minds for clues to who we are, it is like looking at chronologically arranged snapshots in a picture album. We see ourselves, not as we are, but as we were. As Marshall McLuhan says, "We move into the future with our eyes glued to the rear view mirror." Yet, to change, we have to stop seeing ourselves through these old eyes. We have to see who we are, not who we were. *Dig deep into yourself to find your basic essence and tone of being. Who are you?* Answering this question usually requires time and quietness. I once attended a three day workshop that was organized around answering just that simple question. It is not so simple, because there are many layers of personality programming that separate who we really are from who we think we are. Only after many hours and days of intense meditation and psychological processing did the deeper meanings unfold.

Defining your identity comes by learning what lies within your "Sphere of Self." How often do you define yourself by your roles? For example, I'm a writer and a counselor. You are who you are, not what you do. Even if you think you know who you are, it is often difficult to verbalize. Swami Satchidananda said, "Anything you define, you will have to refine, because it was all fine in the beginning." (Fine gold is pure gold.)

Where do you attach your identity? Many people identify with their bodies, which is verified when they say, "I hurt," instead of "My back hurts." Others identify with their emotions and say, "I'm sad," instead of "I feel sad." Still others identify with their mind and say, "I'm smart" instead of "I've got intellengence." **Observe yourself in different situations to see how you react, how you look, and how you use your time.**

This Is Me

When I read that Jean Houston had separated the journey of soulmaking into three stages, I was delighted, for those three stages--This is Me, We Are, and I Am--were exactly the path I had been following. Understanding the first stage, "This Is Me," comes from defining the personality through the personal myth. The astrological archetypes provide an excellent nomenclature for dissecting the personality and learning to distinguish between the many individual subpersonalities vying for attention. Some of our selves work well together, others may be locked in con-flict, but each wants what they want.

Life is a psychological fairy tale, an ever-evolving mystical drama or shadow play, where you are both the star performer and principal audience.

Imagine yourself standing at the center of a temple. The walls of this Temple-of-Being, like those in a funhouse, are large distorted mirrors within which you (the Higher Self) view your several reflections. Each mirror allows only an imperfect view of your true nature. In an attempt to make sense of this variety of subpersonalities, your mind combines them all into a composite called the personality. Because this composite is all you have ever "seen," you accept its structure as real and call the enigma "I."

These mirrors, brought to life by your own interaction with them, are the many god/ess within. These animated beings lie hidden within your psyche as conscious, living spirits. They are the source of your "human nature." The Portuguese poet Fernando Pessoa once said, "In every cor-

personified, your subpersonalities become intelligent life
forms that have voices, points of view, and modes of
action uniquely their own. Each of the god/ess will grant
you various boons and command you to make sacrifices
in their honor. Each will lend you unique powers and
weaknesses.

But, who am i?

The Inner Characters

There are several subpersonalities in my inner cast of characters. One of my strongest selves was my Inner Child, which I named Nelly. When I was younger she was rampant in my life. Although magical, she was also a timid, whiny, little nuisance I called Needy Nelly. Today I am grateful for her, because, by healing her, I found a sense of completeness and gained emotional security. Another subpersonality is Mama Rosa, who wants to control by nurturing and giving. She is like a big breast that tries to feed the world, but she overfunctions and tries to fix things, which often has unfortunate results. The Mama influence on intimate relationships is deadly--she can kill sexuality. Then there is Prudence-Priscilla, my prissy, over-cautious innocent maiden, who is fearful and security-minded. Lusty Loretta is my sexy vamp; Scarlet, my Tantrika. Foxy Roxy is my dynamic performer, who loves creative expression. Sophia is my wise and centered self, and Kami is my consort goddess. There are many faces that make up our psyche.

Think about your subpersonalities. Is there a Clara the Critic, Betty the Biddy, Brunhilda the Bitch, Pitiful Pearl, or Helpless Hanna? Do you know your Wondrous Wanda, Magical Melinda, and your Gorgeous Goddess? Sit down and define the many selves that constellate to form your personality. Begin by giving each a special name, for to control something you must be able to name it. How do your subpersonalities combine and interact to create an executive personality? Who are the dominant players? Which personality is crying for expression by sabotaging your life as a result of neglect?

Who's in Charge?

We wear different subpersonalities, like changes of clothes. We "en-trance" into a web of diverse archetypes. That is why it is so important to know who is in charge. Try to look at every state of consciousness you have ever experienced as a form of trance. Even normal waking consciousness is a type of trance, locking us into a mental energy flow that propels us through life. Our trances form the contents of our classic mind-sets. Each mind-set is like a house, filled with many rooms and stuffed with various contents.

Can you apply this metaphor: "the psyche is a mansion of the mind," and make a connection by examining your own home? See each room as a separate part of the personality.

Our waking trance is only the main floor of our psyche and holds a limited amount of our mind-set. It includes our persona or the mask we wear to the world. Can you see the kitchen as your Caretaker and the living room as your Entertainer? The study is for the Intellect, Critic, and Judge. The office is for the Worker--the writer, counselor, publisher, researcher, real estate agent, whatever. The bedroom is for the Lover. The other rooms may include a place for the musician, audio-visual artist, and a score of archetypical god/ess.

The dark basement represents the unconscious patterns that form the foundation of our being. Here is where we store all our hidden instinctual impulses--our in gences, compulsions and addictions. Memories and imprints from the family come to us through the faces of our Inner Child, the Infant, the fearful Maiden, the Witch, the Savior, and the Beast.

Based upon the sparse contents of the room we inhabit, we form opinions--from moment to moment--about who and what we are. Dreaming is a nightly trance that we enter and, more often than not, we are unaware that there is another self fast asleep in our bed. It is as though the dreaming self had total amnesia. Our waking self may live in the more commodious rooms on the main floor but, like the rooms inhabited by our dreaming self, its "space" is still limited.

Remember, no matter how complete our present trance seems to be, it never holds very much of the total available to us. And, to stress the point: we only know what we experience, the rest we believe. For example, if from birth you had only lived in the kitchen, you would grow up to believe you were a cook. Everything in the kitchen, from the cookbooks to the pots and pans, would confirm that you were a cook. You could seek out all the highest wisdom stored in your room, but the only books available would be about cooking. You would not know any other world.

The Psyche is like a Mansion of the Mind

Who's In Charge, Anyway?

Beware of getting bound to only one subpersonality! Being entranced with just one archetype is like being locked in just one room. Getting out is easy if you know you can, want to, and are prepared to move beyond your limited beliefs.

Changing the Subpersonalities

Our subpersonalities change as we grow. For a while it was Nelly, Priscilla and Mama Rosa running the show. I was a timid woman/child. Needy Nelly's insecurity and shame made me fearful and cautious. Priscilla-Prudence's desire to be liked made me a pleaser who was vulnerable to authority types. Mama Rosa had me running between subservience and bossiness. Rosa finally lost her power when I healed my need to be needed. Awareness of my need to fix things helped me move beyond controlling others. These three, the "Unholy Alliance," as Walter refers to them, dominated my life until I worked through the emotional problems that gave them power over me.

One dream vividly showed me my problem and the solution: Three old biddies were giving me trouble. They threatened to burn my house down. I took them to the top floor and began teaching them to die. If I kept them upstairs they were manageable, but they damaged my upper floor. When I brought them down to the first floor, they were a complete nuisance--always under foot. At best, I could keep them at bay, but guarding them always made me feel like the prisoner. I decide to build them nice basement apartments.

What this dream told me was my three troublesome subpersonalities wanted to live in the attic (the Higher Self), but since the attic and the main floor (the conscious self) were off limits, they really belonged beneath consciousness--somewhere private and hidden. They were part of my past and had once served me admirably but were now holding me back.

When I awoke, I remembered the three old sisters in Agatha Christie's mystery, *Nemesis* . The combined forces of Nelly, Prudence, and Mama Rosa were indeed my nemesis. They were a constellation of all my fears and obsessions that had merged into an aggregate I called "Mama Pris-n-Nelly."

Transforming them was a process of healing the mother, the maiden and the child. Once in meditation, I saw an image from The Wizard of Oz: like the Wicked Witch of the West, water was being thrown on Mama Prisn-Nelly and she was melting, screaming all the way. What changed it for me was to stop letting the child, maiden and mother out in public. Instead, I consciously relate as woman. I have to privately nurture my inner nature, by allowing my loving Mother to honor my Inner Child. I transcend my Maiden's fears when I dare to act and move beyond caring if people like me.

To assist the transition, I had to wake up Dynamic Roxy, Centered Sophia, and my Goddess Kami and make them take center stage. Remember, being a Goddess Warrior calls for dynamic participation in life. It means living in a centered way. It is learning to trust and follow your heart and being committed to operate from love and integrity.

Becoming aware of the forces that pull upon you from within allows room for alternate means of expression. Since the "changing of the guard," I am no longer locked in only a few rooms. Now it is more or less like having the run of the whole castle of the psyche.

We Are

In the second phase of the journey, "We Are," the wisdom of mythology connects us with the archetypical god/ess to explain the phrase "As without, so within." These mythical deities are our inner psychological drives. All god/ess, both good and bad, "live and breathe and know their being" within the collective unconscious.

Jung described the collective unconscious as a constantly moving, ever-changing, deeply hidden consciousness, which lies beneath our normal awareness and underlies, supports, and informs all nature. These unseen networks are the archives that bind all living things together. This web is encoded with the essence of all human development, from the past to the future. It is a well that runs deeper than any individual experience. We are joined, to our benefit or detriment, through our species, our sex, our generation, our society, and our archetypes. The key that releases us from collective bondage is our understanding of the archetypes themselves and our ability to relate their classical myths to our own personal myths.

This book is about invoking the Goddess, for there is a great advantage in awakening our inner powers and partaking of the invisible support of the universe. Invoke the Goddess by imagining that you are walking into different rooms and identifying with different aspects of your archetypical selves. The more you play in these new rooms, the more you will experience their unique wisdom and power. This process opens vistas of creative bliss.

For instance, living with Walter helps me identify with Kami, the Hindu goddess Sivakama, whose name means "the desire that makes creation possible." As the Consort Goddess of Lord Nataraja (Walter's name given in initiation, meaning "universal dancer") I am brought into the cosmic play of creation. As we delve into the Goddess, we open to our creative genius and our houses become mansions and eventually the temples of our souls.

I Am

Despite how substantial these subpersonalities appear to the psyche, the many different selves within these rooms are not the true Self. We have subpersonalities, as we have our children, but they are not us. We are not our bodies. We are not our emotions. We are not our thoughts, nor are we our experiences or the roles we play.

Satchidananda says that we are all actors in a Great Play and God is the Director. In Sanskrit this play is called *Lila* , which means "divine sport." In it, we each have our roles to play with make-up to fit every character. We see all types, yet under the make-up, they are all the same--all aspects of the Goddess. The message of this metaphor is to understand the different masks and outfits we wear. Yet, only when we strip away everything that separates us from others do we learn to identify with our original nature, our Goddess.

In the last stage we identify with "I Am," and learn to live in Grace, as the Spirit of the universe itself. The little selves learn to identify with the Goddess. A Goddess Warrior's challenge is to merge Spirit and matter, Creator and creation.

The quest for self-identity, at every stage of the way, is really the process of identification. We identify with the Goddess by surrendering to the Higher Will--trusting our unfoldment. Truth is revealed through knowing that everything is ordered and cared for by a Higher Power. We are all Goddesses and One in Spirit. Realizing this state is called liberation. It is freedom from bondage to any and all of our different selves.

When we identify with Spirit we live in the present and become an instrument of the Divine, taking no claim as our own. Satchidananda says that when we surrender to the Divine we are no longer like a wild unbroken horse, running after selfish desires, but instead we become a steed for the Divine Rider. We can work efficiently for the good of the whole and all will be provided.

It is the Divine Mother who creates the Goddess Warrior model through me. I reinforce this attitude each day by saying, "Let me be an instrument of Thy Will," for only by awakening to the joy of my Higher Self have I found my grandest vision.

Our Social Myths

Social myths are created from the aggregation of all our personal myths. Although many elements combine to make up a personal myth, its foundation is in our religious background and spiritual beliefs. For me and a vast number of "baby boomers," this framework was a Judeo-Christian Norman Rockwell image of the family supporting both church and state. Walter's myth was just the opposite. His predominant influence was the free wheeling Utopian dream of the flower children who created the "hippie movement" in the sixties. *What myth describes your background?* Each of these modern myths sets a slightly different stage upon which we enact our lives. Each gives us unique boons and individual trials to test our mettle. Society as a whole rises or falls based upon the outcome of each person's quest.

Our collective social myth is patriarchal. We live under an alpha-male system, which believes that a strong, tightly structured government assures survival against threats of destruction and loss of territory. Materialism has become a world religion. The stock market is its temple and financial success, its nirvana. The pressures of modern world economics have shaped today's business ethics to glorify greed and make holy-writ of the corporate policy of bottom line expediency. We have dwelt in the shadow of the threat of nuclear holocaust and the draining of Earth's resources. The U.S. is no longer the sterling symbol of a great democratic nation. To many, Uncle Sam has become a bully who assassinates world leaders and manipulates global markets for his own greedy imperial ends.

Society's problems must first be dealt with on an individual level, for we are all creatures who act as spokespersons for the human family. Society's ills only serve to reflect the consciousness of its people. To identify with the Goddess, an inner healing is essential. Change may be met with great resistance, because changing ourselves is the hardest thing we will ever do--but change we must. Change is made easier when we learn to focus in the moment and remember, "It's a New Age. The time is right and we can make a difference!"

Living the Grand Myth

Despite our current social problems, a Grand Myth is brewing in the cauldron of the human unconscious. We are birthing a consciousness revolution. Since Aquarius is the sign of group consciousness, many believe the second coming of Christ is already here, but that it is a group event. We as a group are learning we are Christ in essence--divine beings.

It behooves us to discover our part in making this New Age a reality. An in-depth exploration of our being is required, for knowledge gained from self-exploration is essential if we are to rely more upon what we know intuitively and less upon what we were taught to believe. *Ask yourself how you can take part in transforming the old and midwifing the new?* By rediscovering the old tools, we can learn to create newer ones. Our challenge is to merge the visionary with the practical, without losing sight of either.

Bridging the gap will take time; the separation is still very deep and wide. Yet rates of change and growth are accelerating through rapid global transportation and communications. The world is growing faster, smaller, and closer than ever before.

Acknowledge yourself as the hero of your own myth. As you learn to understand your personal myth, a newer, more expansive myth evolves by which to live. Campbell says that the swirling, vibrant, blue-and-white photographs of Earth as seen from outer space are our most powerful new mythological images.

When we see the Earth as a globe, we do not see its divisions, only its unity. In this new birth we are one planet, inhabited by one global family.

This transformation will happen only when we stop thinking in parochial terms and awaken to a planetary consciousness. When we become an "ocean frog," we move beyond our little world of personal needs and ambitions and have the sense of being a part of the Great Destiny or Universal Plan.

The Mystery Schools of the ancient Greeks instructed: "Know thyself" and take or do "Nothing in excess." We have to know who we are. We have to know what is our heart's desire. We have to be the very best that we can possibly be, acting with humility and nonattachment to the results of our labor. The simple (but not always easy) way is to sharpen our awareness in each moment, and trust in our own internal energy to guide us.

3

We can have no greater enemy than an untamed mind, and no friend, no mother or father can do as much for us as a well-trained mind.

Buddha

Waking Up Our Awareness

Waking up is the essence of being a Goddess Warrior. Waking up presupposes normal consciousness to be much like dreaming while awake. One of the fundamental principle of Neuro Linguistic Programming (NLP) is that we are always in one sort of trance or another. Our world is a mixture of what is real and what we believe to be real. Our universe can only be seen through the eyes of our belief systems. The mind is a creator, not merely a passive observer. Everything we perceive is screened, sorted, censored, and strained through the machinery of our minds. Mythological teachings have always compared the opening of consciousness to awakening from a profound sleep. That is why Buddha is called "The Awakened One."

Be Here Now

Being a Warrior means overcoming our greatest fears and walking with death as our friend and ally. This is not morbid, it simply implies living each moment as if it were the last. To do this we need dynamic presence. Dynamic presence is the ability to uninterruptedly focus the mind in the moment--the eternal moment--where the only place is here, the only time is now, and the only reality is Self.

Make your motto, Be Here Now. Being "awake" in every moment creates courage, clarity, and strength.

Again, the secret is that "each step is the goal." Only by focusing on our inner pulses do we tap into our wealth of resources and know what is right for us in every moment.

Start by asking yourself, *"What can I do to further my growth in this moment?"* Treat each moment as worthy of your full attention. Approach life with the spontaneity of a child, where everything is new and exciting. Children try everything and examine everything. They do not take things for granted. This attitude is what Buddhists call "the beginner's mind." To enter into your beginner's mind, turn off the auto pilot, release all thoughts unrelated to the present, and become totally fascinated in the moment. In the golden moment there is joy. We can forget time and move beyond fear and desires. There are no ordinary moments for the spiritual Warrior. In *The Way of the Peaceful Warrior*, Socrates exclaims, "You've always tried to be superior in the ordinary, now become ordinary in the superior realm."

Absorbing your entire consciousness into the task at hand makes every activity a dynamic meditation.

To forget yourself in the act of doing is to become what you do. For example, if you paint a picture, you become the entire process--the painter, the painting, and the act of creation. The experience flows, you receive it and allow it to pass. To totally experience a situation or event, you must concentrate and steady your mind. Free yourself from inhibitions, judgments, and ambitions. Set reacha-ble goals so you can wake up your sleepy Watcher, without whose vigilance your mind runs wild.

Awakening the Watcher

The Watcher is a state of awareness. It is called by many names: Witness, Observer, and Bodhi are but a few. It is a part of ourselves that, with practice, will remain totally conscious and focused in the moment even while we engage in intense worldly activity. From this nonattached vantage point, we can observe ourselves joyfully watching life unfold.

The mind's natural state is noisy restlessness. Thoughts continuously rise and fall, skipping and racing everywhere in pursuit of an endless stream of distractions. This state of reverie occurs whenever the mind is on auto pilot. Without the Watcher on duty, our minds toss about like rudderless boats. If committed to writing, the idle chatter that an undisciplined mind generates in a single day would fill volumes. Wouldn't that be a sight to behold?

There are powerful programs operating deep within the more dimly lighted levels of our minds. These programs are the result of prior conditionings that not only distort our perception of reality, but also leave us highly susceptible to the influence of illusion. Like ruts in a road, these mental patterns restrict our freedom of choice and bind us to a system that we cannot see beyond. Just as a frog who lives its entire life at the bottom of a well could never hope to understand the immensity of the ocean, we do not completely understand anything that lies beyond our realm of experience. It is very easy to believe that whatever we think must be true.

A Goddess Warrior learns "the mind makes a good servant but a poor master." Learn to use your mind to create in the moment. Awaken your Watcher by focusing the mind with a gentle, loving hand or it will bog itself down in an endless maze of unimportant details and fantasies.

Try the following exercise with a friend: Stop yourself from using the word "I" in your conversation for an hour. Then spend an hour keeping the conversation in the present, not looking back and not projecting forward.

Playing these games trains the mind to see the Watcher. I am in the habit of not closing closets and cupboard doors, so my lesson is to consciously close them. They offer constant visual feedback on the watchfulness of my Watcher.

The Call for Discrimination

It was recently discovered that women and men have a major difference in the physical structure of their brains. Women have a larger, more complex corpus callosum, a mass of interconnecting ganglia that connects the two hemispheres of the brain. Science can visually see, in living technicolor, three-dimensional scans of information being processed by the brain. An enlarged corpus callosum presumes women have a greater ability to transfer information between the right and left sides of the brain and an improved capacity to co-process information simultaneously in both hemispheres. Computer terms call this "concurrent processing." This suggests there is more information available to women and their sources are more varied. It may mean women have greater capacity for achieving wholeness, but are also more prone to the scatterbrain effect. For women to experience power, they must harness their vast storehouse of available resources.

Our greatest challenge is to think clearly and constructively, and to stop giving so much attention to the mind's frivolous impulses and inclinations.

Our personal universe tends to order itself in conformity with what we, and those around us, believe. As Emerson said, "As a man thinketh, so is he, and as a man chooseth, so is he and so is his nature." Whatever the little self inside believes is what we attract and experience in our daily lives.

Confused and afraid, a client came to me just after discovering she had cancer. She believed that she had created her illness and thought she could cure it. She questioned the need for medical treatment. I told her to reprogram her mind for healing, but also to follow her doctor's advice, because he had a valid part to play in her myth. A year later she invited me to lunch to tell me there were no live cancer cells in her body. She had followed a medical treatment, but believed she had conquered her illness mostly through positively reprogramming her mind.

As we change our thought patterns, we alter our subconscious urges. Just as changing the flow of a stream alters the shape of the riverbed beneath, so does changing the patterns of our thoughts transfigure the fabric of our lives.

How constructive and beneficial are your thoughts? The average mind is filled with countless thoughts. Each by itself is weak, but if focused collectively, thoughts have great power.

Watch the content of your mind throughout the day. Where do you most often place your attention? Take your journal and on the hour, or at least eight times a day, note what you are thinking. Then ask, "Are these thoughts helping my growth? Will they assist me in producing a better life or are they limiting me?" Feel the emotional atmosphere surrounding each group of thoughts. Then categorize your various mental states throughout the day and how long you spend in each mode. If you use a journal and do this exercise diligently, you'll see your Watcher-in-Residence awaken. You will begin to positively direct your quest.

The only way we can get what we want is with a disciplined mind--clear thoughts consciously directed. Remember these simple truths: "Energy follows thought. Whatever we focus upon increases. Whatever we praise expands." The power of positive thinking works! By giving energy to desired results, we bathe our minds in constructive ideas. Your life will unfold in conformity with these thoughts.

Focus on what you want to become, not on what you want to overcome.

Discrimination means focusing clearly on your personal goals and staying in the present to achieve them. Change happens first because of willingness. Say to yourself, "I want to change," and mean it. Next, recondition your past with positive affirmations that begin with, "I am, I can, I do."

Part of my discipline was to spend time each day reciting and writing affirmations to focus on my self-improvement. Here are some of my tried-and-true affirmations that can be used like mantras--said over and over again:

Every day, in every way, I get better and better.

I am Light, I am Love, and I am Goddess.

I am healthy, wealthy and wise.

I am open to receive all that is good for me.

I follow my heart and live in joy.

I awaken my Watcher by Being Here Now.

My mind is eloquently clear and precise.

I trust and surrender to the Divine presence.

All my needs and desires are taken care of.

I enjoy my work, operate at my highest capacity and am well rewarded.

My power increases and so does the love and support in my relationships.

There is power in words. We must become our own "Thought Police." When this book was nearly completed and all that remained was editing, I caught myself telling a friend that "the honeymoon was over." My thoughts were projecting drudgery on that part of the work. Immediately, I saw what I was programming and began to monitor my thoughts more closely. Editing turned out to be quite pleasant, once I extracted the dread from the deed. We must constantly watch what we are creating. When I finally got the truth--that the process was the goal--editing became a joyous journey of refining and clarifying the outer along with the inner.

I had to set goals and watch my subjective mind work, learn not to be affected by my emotions, and surrender to my Higher Self. This process requires patience, gentleness, and awareness in every moment. No matter how confused and undisciplined your mind may be, it can be tamed and transformed. It is just a matter of continuously reminding yourself to come back to the present.

And remember, just as your thoughts form the beliefs out of which your reality is created, everyone's collective thought-forms create the world condition. Therefore the most powerful political action we can take is to promote a positive vision of transformation, world peace, and planetary healing. Speak about that vision with others and do actual physical work to make it happen. There is a new world coming and it is we who will help to build it--one thought at a time.

4

The range of what we think and do is limited by what we fail to notice. And because we fail to notice that we fail to notice, there is little we can do to change, until we notice how failing to notice shapes our thoughts and deeds.

R. D. Laing

Awakening from Maya's Spell

Much of what we believe to be true is not true at all, it is only the present version of what we believe to be true. Because we cannot easily separate ourselves from our observations, our subjective filters distort our view of reality. Life is the Great Illusion that is known in the East as the Goddess Maya. Whenever we are not focused in the present, we are in Maya--the flickering shadowy network of interwoven energy that is full of delusion and deception. Also called Glamour, she is a sweet refrain of the collective that seductively coaxes us to merge with her beauty. She has two connotations. On the one hand, Maya is the effortless beauty of creation. She is inexplicable, spontaneous power; her Divine sport is called Lila. On the other hand she creates the Magic Veil that intoxicates us into believing the fleeting, shifting facades we experience are real.

Of all mystical doctrines, the workings of Maya are said to be the most difficult to grasp. An old Hindu fable illustrates this point:

Hari had been the disciple of a yoga master for years and had diligently practiced every discipline his guru had given him. Hari had learned much and had acquired many yogic powers, but try as he might, he just couldn't grasp the subtle mystery of Maya. Several times he had asked his master to explain this doctrine and each time the explanation left Hari more confused than he was when he arrived. Again, in desperation, he asked his master to explain the mystery. His guru gently smiled, saying, "Yes, Hari, my son, perhaps the time is right. I will try again, but first, go to the river and fetch me some water for I am thirsty."

Hari was off like a shot. He arrived at the river just as the sun was dipping low behind him on the horizon. While he bent over and filled his jug, he looked up and spotted a young woman fetching water from the other side. She looked up at him and smiled. The setting sun fell full upon her face, and as their eyes met, he suddenly saw how truly beautiful she was. She shyly waved, beckoning him to cross over. Without hesitation, Hari waded across to meet her. They exchanged names and glances, and she invited him to dine with her and her family. He agreed and was warmly accepted. As night came he realized that she was the most beautiful and agreeable woman he had ever known. Hari poured out his heart to her, telling her how lonely he had been until he saw her. In that moment he asked her to marry him. She, too, had fallen deeply in love with him and said that she would be proud to be the wife of such a noble man. She said that it did not matter that he was poor because her father had more than enough land for everyone. She knew men of great wealth but had never married because she wanted a man who was as kind and spiritual as herself. Together they ask her father for permission to marry. Her parents were very pleased because Hari was pious and well educated. He was asked to stay and help farm the land, which, in his growing happiness, he did. Within a short time they married.

Time passed quickly. Hari was happy with this wonderful woman. She was as fruitful as she was beautiful. As the years passed they had three children and grew to be very prosperous. They spent their days as though in a dream. It seemed that Hari's happiness could know no limit.

In the fifth year of their marriage the monsoon rains were especially heavy. By Tuesday, a week of rain had filled all the streams and rivers to the point of overflow. It was then that a levee weakened and gave way, sending a mountain of water crashing down upon the village. Fear and panic overtook everyone. With white water raging everywhere, Hari gathered his wife and children and put them all on a large log that would have to serve as their raft. The waters were rampant. Their smallest child was having great difficulty holding on and was soon swept away in the rapids. Hari cried out in terror, his heart breaking as he helplessly watched his youngest child drown.

Just as he thought his heart would burst, a giant wave crashed down upon them carrying off his other two children. His beautiful wife, thinking only of her children, let go of the log in an attempt to save them; all three, crying for help, were pulled under. Hari jumped from the log desperately swimming to rescue them but could do nothing! He watched his dearly beloved wife with the last of their children, disappear into the raging white water. He finally bumped violently against the shore and dragged himself out. He was half dead himself, his entire mind filled with the desperation of his great loss. He collapsed, sobbing in grief and exasperation, but amidst the wail of his anguished cries he heard the sound of a kind and familiar voice softly saying, "Where is the water, my son? Have you forgotten me? You've been gone for nearly an hour."

Hari's "mind trip" is an example of the melodramas we live all the time. It shows how we become totally identified with the thought forms of our minds and become swept in the power of illusion. In a dream state we can do anything, for time and space blend. Life becomes a "magic picture show of the mind." Everyday becomes a dream with which we identify. We project our fantasy world outside, because we are convinced it is real. Maya's illusions fuel the sport of Lila.

Glamour sweeps us into her web. She seeks to lull us into a dreamlike state of consciousness, happily playing her games. Maya's spirited ways want to create. My imagination loves to play in her flowing creation. Perhaps Maya's magical hand helped weave the stories in this book? It is our divine right to create. We must all do so, as unique expression of the Divine, and become love-based co-creators with the Goddess.

Seeing Beyond Maya's Entrancements

Maya entrances us with fantasies, daydreams, television, movies, music, romantic novels, and drugs. She tantalizes us with image magnifiers, fame and fortune, and psychic powers--goodies she presents us with in order to distort our reality. Maya temporarily sidetracks us through her enchantments, ambitions, self-interest, and material desires. When we forget that we are loving co-creators with the Goddess, and dwell continually upon these enchantments, we are plagued with fear-based survival issues, feelings of doubt, "spaciness," and depression.

Without awareness, Maya diverts us from our true path--the heart of the Great Mystery. Our true purpose is to seek the Pearl of Great Price, the Bliss of unity with the Divine Mother. Identify with the Goddess, the All There Is. Be one with Cosmic Consciousness.

What thoughts or fears keep you separate from this blissful unity? One of my friends realized she feared she would lose of her sweet and well-meaning personality. She found herself contracting at the thought of loss. This issue was then mirrored in her husband's fear of her getting lost in spiritualism.

Every person who diligently treads the path will eventually reach the goal of identification with the Divine Mother and will automatically tap into her Wisdom and Light. We can take as long as we need to come to Her, but to do so, we must awaken from the spell of Illusion, or the splendor of the Divine Goddess will always remain hidden.

Try to understand Maya by imagining the Divine Mother dwelling on the top of a high mountain, her throne a shower of brilliant lights. Ascending the steep and winding pathway, which leads to her source, is often described as "walking the razor's edge." This path passes through the neon reality of our cities, across the wilderness, over deep waters, and beyond the valley of surrender. Maya's Magic Veil and colorful forms hide the Divine Mystery. Through our distractions we are misled down the aimless mountain highways and are kept dancing to the beat of Lila, her Divine Sport. And yet, if we were to finish too quickly, who would remain to play in her Lila?

Penetrating Illusion

Awakening discrimination is cutting through our lack of understanding and blindness caused by clouded thinking. Learning to focus, meditate and pray are ways to transcend the ever-present Grand Illusion.

Our minds have been equated to a pond whose surface is whipped into waves of activity by the storms of our emotions. Just as the surface of the pond is in intimate contact with the air above, every thought has a parallel emotional component. When our minds are lashed by emotional storms, our visions are limited to our view of the ripples. To see within our depths, where our true nature can be known, we must ultimately calm our emotions and identify with universal consciousness. Ramakrishna said, "To understand this, imagine you are a salt doll going down to measure the depth of the ocean."

Whatever we believe with our minds, no matter how profound the knowledge, no matter how true it rings, no matter how many others believe it, it is only a belief. Unless we are ruthlessly honest with ourselves, we believe what we are taught and see only what we want to see. This Zen saying is as a way to see beyond illusion:

First there is a mountain, then there is no mountain, then there is.

For the average person, a mountain is just what it is--a big mound covered with trees and rocks. But when curiosity overcomes disinterest one is finally compelled to climb the mountain and have a closer look. As we climb we see only the path and a limited area around us. When we reach the top we see it as a mountain again. So it is as we explore our spiritual path.

The world is rich in opportunities to make continual discoveries, but in our quest for understanding, we lose sight of the one in our zeal to know the many. We miss the mountain, but see a multitude of details, causes and effects, that can only be symbolically understood. When we open to our personal myths and investigate archetypes, we find our lives linked synchronistically with deeper universal patterns. Things that were obscured before can now be seen more clearly. Within our ever-active minds, our journey is transformed into a masterwork of miasma, filled with technical and mystical phenomena.

The deeper we look into the meaning of life, the more we are naturally overwhelmed by its complexity. No matter how confusing it all becomes there is only one thing to remember: Ultimate reality is composed of only two elements-- the thing in itself and whatever we happen to think about it. What we think about something must always be suspect, for nobody's mind can hold it all, and the only way we understand anything is to become it. Only after all the thinking and talking about the meaning of life do we experience it just as it is. It is a mountain again, only this time, it is warmer and friendlier because we penetrated its mystery and shared its secret.

5

Integrity is a willingness to spontaneously go along with truth regardless of other people's choices or opinions.

Buckminster Fuller

Awakening Integrity

Waking up is the essence of the Adventure. It is a mission that is simple to learn but difficult to do. Not only do we live within the spell of the all-pervasive veil of illusion, but we are conditioned into a trance by past patterns and beliefs. Their sleepy webs ensnare us automatically--but there is a way out.

Sleeping Beauty

"Sleeping Beauty," is an allegory about the awakening of consciousness that has withstood the test of time. As the story goes:

There was a king and queen who, after many years of trying, finally had a baby daughter, whom they named Beauty. They were so pleased with their good fortune, that they invited everyone to their palace for a celebration--everyone, that is, except the Queen of Evil.

The three good fairies came, each bearing a gift for the princess. The first fairy gave her beauty, the second, a golden voice, but just as the third fairy was about to give Beauty her gift, the dark queen burst in unannounced, her mouth dripping this curse: "...by the age of sixteen she will prick her finger on a spindle and die." The third fairy wanted to intervene, but could not entirely undo the evil curse. She could, however with her magical powers reduce the impact of Beauty's misfortune. She proclaimed that Beauty would not die by the spindle's prick, but would only sleep until true love could awaken her.

As predicted, the Prince, armed with the shield of virtue and the sword of truth, finds Beauty's castle and does battle with the Queen of Evil. In the fight, he loses the shield of virtue, but conquers evil with the sword of truth. Then the Prince kisses Beauty and consciousness and light return to all the land.

This curse can be compared to being conditioned from birth to sleep in a trance of limitation and ignorance. The good fairies represent potencies of our Higher Selves. They are our Goddess powers, our creative genius, our resources. These powers cannot totally undo evil, but can modify it to produce a positive outcome.

When the princess was a child she lived a sheltered life. She was not allowed to spin, i.e., to live and work within the world where she would certainly experience desire and attachment. The Hindu/Buddhist tradition teaches that attachment leads to the sleep of ignorance. Before adolescence the princess lived completely in harmony with nature and at peace with the golden voice of her Higher Self. She lived entirely within her dream-world, immersed in profound innocence.

As adulthood awakened within her, she began to desire sexual union. This joining represents her completion, for she embodies the full flowering of love. She is your heart's desire. The prince is a symbol for the will, for Divine Will is needed to awaken Divine Love. The kiss that Beauty awaited was the embrace of her own self-love.

In "Sleeping Beauty," truth conquered evil. It has been said that when all else fails, "The truth will set you free," yet to experience truth, we must embody it. Without integrity, we fail to reach pure love and the curse will continue to weave its sleepy web. Every breach of integrity creates discord. Discord causes pain, and pain drains our energy and clouds our minds.

Patsy's Story

Patsy is a vivid example of how runaway desires can breach integrity and bind the soul. Patsy came to me regularly and, although she heard my counsel, she rarely took my advice. She was like a recalcitrant daughter whom I helplessly watched sink deeper and deeper into an abyss of torment. Like a moth, she seemed compelled to fly into the flame. I told her repeatedly, "Life just doesn't work when you are out of integrity. Relationships do not last without integrity."

Patsy is very female, a submissive little-girl type who is lovable and sweet but very self-destructive. When she came to me she was involved in a year-long affair with her neighbor Larry, while both were involved in a primary relationship at home. Her affair began as a little thing, but in time it grew into a major obsession because she had became erotically fixated with Larry. The intrigue surrounding the affair only fueled the fire--it made her feel alive. As time passed she started pulling away from her live-in lover, George, and gravitated toward greater entanglement with Larry. Eventually, her whole life was caught up in lies. She told one story to George, one to Larry, another to her friend Rebecca (Larry's lover), a variation on George's theme to her mother, and yet another tale to her friends. Sound confusing? As her counselor and main confidant, I can testify that it was.

At first this juggling act was difficult for Patsy, but the more she broke with integrity, the easier it became. Of course, walking a tightrope is not without stress. To cope she began drinking regularly, which in time grew to become a serious problem. About the same time, she started working in a doctor's office where she gained easy access to drugs. Soon she found herself habituated to amphetamines as well as alcohol and headed for complete emotional breakdown.

Patsy's weakness grew stepwise from a lack of basic integrity. Each little lie seemed less painful than the full weight of the truth, but each new infraction added power to those that had gone before, further cementing her iron-clad need for more subterfuge. Finally her energy was drained and her house of cards fell. The affair was over. Shortly after that she separated from George. She was out of work, an alcoholic, hooked on "uppers," emotionally spent, and completely lacking in self-respect. Patsy deeply regretted the whole affair with Larry. She wanted to patch things up with George. She needed to find peace, so she decided that, all else having failed, she wanted to try living in truth. She decided that living in truth meant telling everything, so she did. Was it love or guilt that motivated her to tell George all the gory details? As two years of betrayal poured out, George became furious. He finally struck her and left for good. Patsy's sad tale shows that although we can have most of what we want, some pleasures just hurt too much to be worth the price we have to pay.

When we are involved in telling lies or having affairs, our minds are busily locked up in intrigue. As Shakespeare said, "Oh what a tangled web we weave when first we practice to deceive." Lies lead to intrigue and to melodrama, and melodrama is an excellent way of keeping life frivolous. Our personal soap operas assure us that we can continue to avoid getting at the real meaning of life.

Goddess Warriors need to abandon unethical models of living. Ethical perfection is the foremost requirement, not an elective. Ethical perfection is self-imposed integrity, based upon an impeccable code of behavior. We must see that honesty is carved in our personal life and practiced at all times.

The easiest breach of integrity is lying. We learned it as children, as a way to gain power through communication. We have to refuse any benefit this unethical power may bring. Opportunities to bend the truth are often little tests that the universe designs to help us overcome our weakness. I believe integrity is the price we pay for grace. If we try to live without the sword of truth and still pursue self-improvement, life just will not work. Without integrity there is no endurance, because we are out of alignment with the universe. Remember, we cannot live to our fullest potential, let alone win the prize of higher consciousness, without embodying truth. Our challenge is to bring the highest part of ourselves, our Divine Presence, into every aspect of our lives.

Patsy was a difficult case for me. She could not live her truth because she was trapped by her desires. I worked with her for more than a year and I felt completely ineffectual. I finally told Patsy that she should get into a substance abuse treatment program and start seeing another counselor. It was sad. I thought I had lost her, or rather that is what I thought when I first wrote her story.

Integrity is the Price You Pay for Grace

Some time later, Patsy called and her words were music to my ears. She said it had been five months since she had a drink. She thanked me for all the help I had given her and said, "I guess I had to hit rock bottom before I could understand what you meant. But now I'm trusting and surrendering to the Divine. I've learned that when you live in truth and trust God, life takes care of itself." Patsy has been in a rehabilitation center, working with an AA program. She told me about her problem and how bad it had become. She had become a maintenance drinker who started early in the morning and continued building momentum until she would finally pass out at night. For a while she was filling two garbage bags a week with empty wine bottles. That is when she decided to economize and start on hard liquor.

But now, with enthusiasm in her voice Patsy says, "It's so wonderful to feel alive again. People are telling me how confident I seem." I asked her if she was in a relationship. She answered, "Not now. I want all the emphasis to be on my growth." She was interviewing for a substance treatment staff job. She said, "I hope to use my experience and help others with their integrity and addiction problems." Then she said, "I wish I could hug you." "Your phone call is more than a hug," I replied, "I am so happy for you." When I hung up, I spontaneously yelled, "Yeah, Patsy!" It was another sign of the Divine at work.

Living With Love and Integrity

A Goddess Warrior creates behind the badge of love and integrity. To love means to value and accept yourself unconditionally without judgment. Love means to trust your heart's desire to find what you love to do, and then take action toward doing it. You do not have to focus on changing yourself, instead you need to deepen your compassion and vitalize your inner Light. Our life's purpose is to become a loving Light. Shine your Light and let others shine theirs.

Integrity means living by three basic rules: truth, fairness and harmlessness. Can you imagine how different this planet would be if everyone followed these simple rules? Build your integrity through a commitment to honesty, by keeping your agreements and dedicating your life to perfect action.

Perfect Action

It is your responsibility to perform only those actions that are worthy. Truthful words and clear thoughts, blen-

Love and Integrity is the Goddess Warrior's Shield

ded with a conviction for harmlessness, leads to right action. Karma can be compared to Newton's law of inertia/momentum which states, "A body at rest tends to remain at rest and a body in motion tends to remain in motion at the speed and direction in which it is traveling." Every decision initiates action. Every action begins as thought and is clothed in words before ever becoming a deed. What you do now sets your course and generates the forces that propel you into the future. When you do a Christlike action--in that moment, you are Christ.

Perfect action requires proper decision-making tools. A basic guideline is to ask, "Does this action cause harm (physically, mentally, emotionally or spiritually) to me or others?" If an action causes no harm and has the possibility of doing some good, then it is probably a perfect action.

Once we learn to remove ourselves from the spell of our periphery desires and choose integrity, the Goddess can make contact with its form. In the fairy tale of "Sleeping Beauty" this is when the Prince kisses Beauty. When Prince, as pure Will, functions over pure Love, an alchemical awakening occurs. As we develop our will, consciousness becomes infused with Spirit, and new life and awareness spread throughout our psyche.

6

Building an Enlightened Will

Awakening female power activates woman's will in the world. Develop your will so you have the energy and fire to carry out your purpose. The power of your individuality is experienced in terms of your will. Roberto Assagioli, the founder of Psychosynthesis, said, "The will is the function which most relates to the self. It is purpose based on intentionality, valuation and motivation." It is being deliberate and using discrimination to make decisions. To say "I will do this" creates a clearly focused direction toward that end, so if you want a better world, you must be willing to help create it. Remember, "If there is a will, there is a way."

Ragnel and Gawain

The riddle within the myth of Ragnel and Gawain is a pearl of wisdom containing great truth.

One day while King Arthur was hunting in a forbidden neighboring kingdom, he was confronted by a large dark knight who threatened to kill him. Arthur pleaded for leniency, saying, "I am king, it would not be wise to kill me. What do you want?" The Dark Knight said he would spare the king, if he could solve this riddle:

"What is it that woman wants most?"

If not answered within a year, Arthur would be hanged. Gawain was the most noble and gallant knight of the round table, and it was to him that Arthur turned in his hour of need. When Arthur explained his plight, Gawain volunteered to "scour the kingdom" and survey everyone who might know the answer.

Near the end of a fruitless year the king met an ugly, disgusting witch in the woods. Her name, it seems, was Ragnel. She scowled and told him he was in deep trouble. She said she had the answer that would save him, but there was a price: She would share her wisdom with Arthur, but in return he must force the most virtuous of his knights to marry her.

You think I'm a hag, but I'm a Lady!

Arthur could hardly believe his ears or his eyes. This witch lent new dimension to the connotation "ugly!" She slobbered and stank, and was completely appalling in looks and manners.

Arthur was so bewildered that he just stood there gaping at her. How could he command the best of his knights to marry someone so repulsive! He finally said, "I cannot do that to any of my knights." "Very well for you," Ragnel croaked, "You may think I"m a hag, but I'm really a lady." Then the witch demanded, "Go now! Tell Gawain that your life is in his hands."

When told, Sir Gawain willingly offered to do anything to save his king. When the year was up the Dark Knight appeared before Arthur. "Well?" he thundered, "It's time for your answer. . . Or your life. . . Which is it to be?" Answers from the survey were given, but none satisfied the Dark Knight. Finally, in desperation, Arthur uttered the answer supplied by the witch.

"Women most want sovereignty over their own lives."

It was the right answer. Arthur then had to fulfill his promise. With this, Ragnel jubilantly announced she wanted a royal wedding and a castle-wide celebration. The king's attendants tried to talk her out of it, but there was no way to dissuade her from her desires. Ragnel and Gawain married. The people of Camelot were sad. They could not bear even to look upon her, for Ragnel was that horrible.

On their wedding night, Ragnel told Gawain that he must make love to her in all her ugliness. He dutifully marshaled all his courage, bent over, and kissed her. When their lips met he felt a strange sensation. As he stood there looking at her, she slowly changed into a beautiful young woman.

She smiled at him and said, "Because you were willing to love me, the spell has been removed, but only part way. Now I am to be ugly only half the day. Dear knight, you must now choose. If you wish, I can be beautiful only during the day. With this choice you will win the admiration of others, but at night your private time will be spent with a witch. If you want me beauti-

ful at night I will bring you great pleasure but you'll
face the pity and scorn of the entire kingdom."

The wise Gawain stood looking at the most charming woman he had ever known and said, "I accept you
for who you are. Therefore, I must ask you what it is
you want to be, for the most I can ask is that you
simply be yourself."

Giving me the choice has released me!

Upon hearing his words, she rejoiced, "Thank you. Because you have given this choice to me, you have released me from the rest of the spell."

Rumor has it, they lived happily ever after.

This tale shows us that the Witch inside us must be acknowledged. "Witch consciousness" is when we catch ourselves feeling sickly, old, or terrible, but also righteous. Remember, Ragnel said, "You may think I am just a disgusting hag, but I'm really a lady." When caught in her spell, you must never forget who you really are.

You transform the Witch by loving, accepting, and giving her sovereignty over herself.

The story tells us to trust the Witch, despite everyone's reaction to her--scorn, criticism, disgust, and feelings of dutiful dread. Just stay with her. Trust the female to save the inner kingdom. Ragnel chose and the king was spared. It is our intuitive female side that must be allowed to take the lead, for therein lies the inspiration of our heart's desire. Gawain, who represents the animus, received what he ultimately wanted by giving up conscious control. His action transported him from a relationship of obligation to one of inner union and joy.

Successful Self-Assertion

Women most want to rule over their own lives. To awaken female power, we must assert what's right for us. This means letting our words and behavior express the flow of our feelings. Communicate openly and directly with people. Express your needs and desires. Find your Witch, for she can help you stick to your principles and convictions and live your virtues.

The key to successful self-assertion is knowing the source of your inner desires. Do things because you want to do them, not to fulfill obligations and expectations. Do not do anything because you'll feel guilty or anxious if you don't. Do it for yourself rather than just to please others. Use your own judgment to decide what you want to do with your time and energy. In the long run, it is never easier to remain passive and do things against your will. You pay for it with a lack of aliveness.

Look within to what you really want and take a stand despite appearances. Speak in a kind but firm voice without being antagonistic or challenging. Caution: Don't dump negative feelings on others or express your feelings in a tantrum.

Assertion says, "I want what I want and I am aware of your desires too." It promotes intimacy. Aggression, on the other hand, says, "I want what I want and I don't care about you," which creates separation.

Rights are something we give ourselves and that means more than simply "fight or flight." We can confidently take the initiative, and armed only with daring and courage, reach for our objectives. Let us stop waiting for things to happen, but instead, become the cause. By getting into the driver's seat, we learn to step out and enroll others into "our thing." The more we assert what we feel, the more power we have.

Becoming Decisive

Decisiveness stems from knowing who we are and what we want. The question is how do we make clear decisions when there are so many possible choices and so many subpersonalities vying for the power to make them--let alone other people's opinions.

The fuel of life is everywhere. Our free will propels us to be creators.

Each decision involves tradeoffs. We have to say "No" to what we don't want, in order to leave room for what we do want.

We continually face decisions that have the power to advance us or lead us astray. Clarity comes by asking, "What will bring me the greater joy?" In order to find a clear vision, examine the facts and weigh the consequences. Check your feelings and intuition. Our choices need to reflect our own special style. In difficult decisions, we may need the opinion of others, but the final decision must come from ourselves. By expanding our inner awareness and freeing the mind of fear, we can suspend its idle chatter and let our inner resources show us the way.

It's not good to always change your mind, but it is your right. After a decision, it is best to stop thinking about it, but if you can't, you may need to look deeper and consider again.

Being Your Own Authority

Become your own authority. Take the power and become the author of your own story.

First ask yourself: Do I let others tell me what to do? To whom do I give my power? What gives others control over me? Am I being trained by subtle control methods, through guilt, judgment, passive aggression, or patterns of obligation? How do I allow my "should's, cannot's, and if only's" to rule my life?

We have authority when we listen to ourselves and do not look to others for our validation. We are an authority, when we accept ourselves as adults and stop thinking that everyone else knows better. We become an authority when we trust ourselves and remember the goodness and wisdom of the Goddess at our core. The answers we seek are within. Our big lesson is to learn to trust our own feelings, which demands that we get clear and know what we want. We have to "hold our own" against other people's strong opinions.

Finding the Motivation Behind Will

Only strong emotional energies can spur our will forward. There must be a motivation to work, a higher purpose. Look to your heart for guidance and know that the cue is love. Campbell says we find our purpose by finding our bliss, that deep sense of being in joy. It is a push that comes from within.

If you are doing what your heart wants to do, you will be living in love and joy. If you believe you are doing what you were "cut out" to do, but are miserable doing it, you have probably ignored your inner promptings. Relax and learn to let the Goddess flow through you to find your real purpose--the source of your deeper needs, the roots from which the tree of your destiny grows.

Quietly look within and answer these questions: How can I be of service? What is my unique purpose? What do I love to do? What do I want to do? Be detailed and specific. Do I have a natural ability? Will it bring me joy? As I examine my wants, what are my deep heart's desires? What are my highest aspirations? What motivates me to want those desires? Do my motivations serve my highest good? What does life require of me? What is my responsibility to myself, to my family, to my community, and to the world?

My deep inner push was my fascination with human behavior. At a young age I was told I was full of "kitchen philosophy." Actually, I am a keen observer, a great list maker, love to talk, and have a burning desire to serve others. These natural abilities led me first to counseling, and then to teaching, coaching, and story telling, which naturally led me to joy. My strongest ambition is identification with the Cosmic Mother. Recognizing this heartfelt motivation serves to ignite my passions and inspires me further.

Embracing the Heroic Urge

The heroic journey is about coming into your own. It means believing in yourself. It means having the guts to follow your heart, venturing out into the unknown, never knowing, but always trusting, that the doors will open. Trust is the main lesson,but an old Sufi adage tells how: "Pray and then tie the horse." Pass beyond your old beliefs, and with faith and conviction, take down-to-earth measures.

Follow your heart's desires, and make sure you take practical steps and ground yourself in the real world.

Creating my job in the world was a big part of my visionary quest. What a journey! For years I questioned, "How should I live my life?" After being totally disillusioned in the business world, I discovered that I had two desires. I wanted to learn metaphysics and I wanted to see the world, so I became a flight attendant. I spent a decade flying the friendly skies, all the while seeking knowledge. When I was in my late twenties, I announced to my suitor, who was very practical and traditional, that

I had decided to become a metaphysical counselor. He was stunned. "Do you know anyone that is one?" I smiled a nervous, "No." Then he said, "Can you make a living at that?" I didn't know, but I really wanted it and a big part of me believed I could have it. Well, I bid my boyfriend, "Goodbye," quit flying, and hung out my shingle. Everyone I knew thought I was lost to magical thinking. Concerned friends advised me not to let go of my nice secure job. I confess I had more than my share of doubts and stomach aches. My security based subpersonalities were rarely comfortable the first few years. I found it necessary to stay away from people who reinforced my doubts. Timid, alone, and afraid, my heroic urge pulled me onward to make it on my own and I've never had to get another job.

Bringing the Will to Form

Once we know what we want, we have to learn how to go about getting it. All the myths tell us that heralds will come and the doors will open. Actually when our desires remain conscious, opportunities present themselves.

One of my early clients said, "You're wonderful, and I'll help you, but you'll need a miracle to make it." The universe supported my discipline and determination. Within a year, I was lecturing, had an adequate client load, and was writing an astrological self-growth newspaper column. When we find what we love to do the money follows. So, go for what you want! Believe in yourself and be persistent. If you try, you will be able to contribute to life in your own special way.

List what you can do to actualize your Shining Self and become the Guardian of your destiny. What are some things you will do as soon as you can? How can you nurture and develop your talents? Are there any new books, training or skills that you need to accomplish your goals?

It is important to develop the skills necessary to do worth-while work. There is so much that needs to be done. For me, taking a simple typing course opened a whole new career. I never learned typing in high school or college, but finally gave myself the ability to fulfill my heart's desire and become a writer by committing to a few easy lessons. It was so simple, I wondered why I had resisted it for so long.

Without firmly directing your will, random thoughts will lead you down paths that are scenic but unproductive. My ally was discrimination. I had to retrain my mind, and learn to control my thoughts. I continually affirmed that my livelihood was the right choice. I kept saying, "My intuition will show me the way to unfold my success." I worked hard to reprogram my thoughts, my feelings and my actions. I would not allow fearful reveries about failure to enter my sphere of influence. By the magic of synchronicity, my clients continually mirrored what I was learn-ing. I've been my biggest client, teaching myself what I needed most to learn.

Persistence is another characteristic of will.
We cannot fail, if we never quit.

Constantly work to become conscious, to disregard the limiting images, beliefs, and conditionings, and make the process the goal. It takes focus, patience, and one-pointedness to overcome all obstacles. Your power comes by being in the present.

Once we have purpose and dedication, vision follows naturally. We must learn to express our visions, since they are not just for us alone.

Developing Practice

We cultivate ourselves and strengthen our will through some sort of practice. Devote time and energy to training your mind and moving toward your goals, for it is the most crucial step in self-growth. Only with regular practice can we take the knowledge of ourselves and our limitations and make our lives worthwhile.

Deliberation is needed, especially in the beginning. Like building muscles, working with the will develops and strengthens us. Simple exercises of the will like walking each day or not eating between meals can be a powerful tool. Listening to your feelings non-judgmatically and expressing them properly in the present is a powerful practice to gain balance. I've learned that my daily routines of physical exercise and meditation are my anchors in the seas of life. They keep me on center.

Make it your practice to live in harmony with the Goddess by being thoughtful of the Earth.

The most basic way to love the Goddess is respecting the Earth. **Do you defile her or waste her resources?** If you don't recycle papers, glassware, aluminum and tin cans, and if you are not sparing with your plastic consumption, you are throwing it all away. If possible, make compost out of your organic matter, and plant flowers, vegetables and trees. Only you can create the world you want, so if you want a better future, will it--visualize it, enlist sup-port, and work to make it happen. "Think globally, act locally."

Expressing the Right Use of Will

Consciously choose the direction as well as the object of your will. This demands taking responsibility for both the pleasure and the price of obtaining your desires. Our soul becomes bound to the objects of our desires, so if our desires prove unworthy, we will be pulled from grace. Search for your heart's desire. It will reflect the Light of your Source.

Life is a co-creation with the Divine. We need a strong sense of personal will, for it is the drive toward perfection that brings results. Bear in mind that this is an inwardly directed use of will. We have, by divine right, absolute dominion over only one person--ourselves. If we wish to create in this world, we need to remember the good of all and do so like a musician playing in a symphony. We must tune our instruments to the same pitch and play the same score as the Goddess. We remain synchronized by paying close attention to the Conductor, taking our cues from our inner nature, and playing our lead only when it is appropriate. We must trust that if we do not get our heart's desire, the Goddess has a better part for us to play. Choose again, practice, and then audition.

To have a joyful, satisfying life upon the quest, we are asked to consciously surrender. If our intent is an enlightened will we need to add, "If it is Thy Will and my highest purpose, let it be."

The universe painfully teaches us that, "to have the object of our desire we must be willing to let it go." If it is of real importance, it will return on its own. The road of evolution is often traveled by the vehicle of insecurity.

Although, when we live in harmony with the Goddess, we do not have to concern ourselves with what we will be, what we will do, or what we will have. All will be provided.

A simple Goddess Warrior code is :

Have the courage to ask for what you want, despite appearances, but don't be attached to the results.

II. BE CENTERED

7

Balancing Duality

Duality is the very nature of the universe. Our solar system sits in the cold dark periphery of our galaxy, out beyond a dust cloud that cuts us off from the heat and light of galactic central. Here the rotation of the earth on its axis creates extreme differences between night and day. From the time we first open our eyes, life breaks up into an endless chain of lighted activity and darkened unconsciousness.

The universal interplay of polar opposites is all pervasive. Positive-negative, conscious-unconscious, yin-yang, light-dark, and male-female, the Goddess and the beast are all aspects of the greater whole. Here is an old Scottish fairy tale that describes the nature of our adventure in duality:

Once two sisters were traveling on a mountain. One climbed upward, lifted by a long golden thread tied to a celestial crane that soared high overhead. The other was descending, dragged along by a big black dog chained to her by an iron leash.

One day their paths crossed and they stopped to compare journeys. They shared stories about the dangers they had faced: the uncertain weather, the steepness of the climb, wild animals, and avalanches. They also told of their joys and pleasures, such as warm sunshine, fresh air, beautiful flowers, and incredible vistas. They enjoyed each other's company so much that they agreed to travel together from that point onward.

They started off, intending to walk together, but soon found it pretty heavy going because they were being pulled in totally opposite directions. The descending sister, who was bound to her beast by an iron chain, could not break away no matter how hard she tried. The ascending sister, seeing that her descending sister could not break free and climb with her, decided to cut her delicate golden cord to travel with her sister. After all, she thought, "Some companionship is better than none at all. And besides, I have given my word."

So she cut her golden cord and the two went off together. But without the crane to guide and help her over the steeper places, the ascending sister soon lost her way. After a while she realized her dilemma, but by then it was too late--there was no way out for her. She knew she could not continue to take directions from the descending sister because she would be led to certain destruction in the pit below. She tried to retrace her steps and regain her original direction but could not tell which way was up. It had been so easy to sever her golden cord, but now she had to face living as a disconnected person, condemned to wander aimlessly. She finally became a bad spirit, eternally guarding a gaping crevasse. Unable to ascend or descend, she was caught in eternal limbo, a state of being Buddhists call the "realm of the hungry ghosts."

The mountain symbolizes the world. The sisters are the dual aspects of our human nature.

We are both a soaring spirit and a raging beast. We have both an angel and a demon. We are children of matter as well as the Goddess.

If we separate from our spiritual source, we will become an empty shell--a wraith without higher purpose. The lesson of the two sisters is glaringly obvious--protect your connection to the Higher Self at all cost. It is a delicate, sensitive vibration that only you can break, and only through an act of your own will.

Finding the Spiritual Source

Embrace the higher intelligence of the Goddess, that is within everyone and everything. Just as planting a seed is the prerequisite for picking the flower, finding your spiritual Source is the essence of the Great Work. Most people feel separate. They do not realize that they exist within a great Unity, and this ignorance creates a fragmentation in their being. Ignorance means to ignore the truth.

Once, when I had recurring headaches, I asked the universe for a sign. That night I had a dream: I was visiting with an astronaut when news came announcing the death of the "flyboy" Atman (Atman is the Sanskrit name for the Higher Self). When I awoke, I realized that I was caught up in the mundane world. I was letting my material desires direct my mind and was neglecting to tend the spiritual garden that was my temple of Atman. I changed my ways and rarely get headaches anymore, but when I do it serves as a reminder. As we learn to align and flow with our Spirits, we open ourselves to all the good this universe has to offer.

The art of soulmaking demands that we release ourselves from who we think we are and open ourselves to the greater Unity of who we really are.

Our highest purpose is to become a luminous source of Light, a living Christ. As Jesus said, "Ye are the Light of the world." How can we say with conviction that "I am a Goddess" when our behavior makes liars of us? Our divinity is hidden by the denser qualities of our personalities, just as a lantern coated with soot cannot radiate the light within. Thoughts, driven by desire, stir up the mind and distort what can be seen within. We need to get the distractions out of the way and allow the Higher Self to shine through.

Yet, as we strive toward wholeness, our personalities exert a powerful hold. They maintain the illusion of separateness by continually reasserting past patterns onto our present behavior. The voice of the beast is potent, but that of the Higher Self is a whisper. This fact is easily seen in music: When a stringed instrument is "open tuned" and a bass note is plucked, its vibrations overwhelm the natural tendency of the higher treble strings to remain at rest. But inversely, when a treble string is plucked, there is hardly any movement in the bass strings. The power that drives our lower or baser nature is a strong physical force that masks our higher nature like a solar eclipse hides the sun.

We cultivate our connection to the Goddess by training our minds, for only a well-disciplined mind can influence its lower nature. The spirit does not have the power to lift us unless our beast is light and well behaved. The beast will not be ignored, and cannot always be coddled. The difference between a "good" dog, who gives love and emotional warmth and a "bad" dog, who brutally drags us down the mountain, is a matter of being master-ful.

Training the Beast

The beast is our instincts, created from the individual cellular consciousnesses that make up our bodies. The prime directive of the beast is survival, first as an individual, then as a troop, and finally as a species. If you feel "I must have it," you are coming from survival. The pursuit of pleasure and the avoidance of pain assure our survival.

The beast is either an ally or an enemy, depending upon how it behaves. The face of the beast takes many forms. Fear, illusion, flightiness, overindulgence, laziness and envy are only a few. It is easy to see the face of the enemy. Just set a goal and watch the barriers appear that prevent you from reaching it.

In spite of the fact that it is your soul's adversary, try to think of your "beastie" affectionately. After all, it is your faithful companion. Your relationship to your beast is like a warrior riding upon the shoulders of a gorilla. Sometimes, all you have to do is tell the gorilla what to do or which way to turn, and it is instantly done. But at other times, nothing seems to work. The beast just "has a mind of its own." Have you ever looked back upon an action and said, "Whatever possessed me to do that?" Have you ever thought before sitting down to a holiday dinner, "I'll just eat a little," only to helplessly watch yourself fall into a full feeding frenzy?

Seeing the Face of Your Beast

To help you along, quickly and without much thought, name three animals. After you have written down three of God's creatures, examine their specific qualities. See if their behavior mirrors how you see yourself or how others see you.

Is your beast friend or foe? Is it always looking for bananas? Is it always struggling to get more?

Name your animal totem. Shamans believe they are your inner potencies--spirits that offers you strength.

Training the beast is much like housebreaking the family dog. Lasting changes in behavior take time and patience, and always proceed more quickly with appropriate rewards and punishments. Indulging your beast is like walking it with a large rubber band instead of a leash. It will still drag you wherever it wants, it just takes a little longer to know you are in trouble. Furthermore, you can't kill your beast or chain it to a post in the back yard. You've got to eat with it, sleep with it, and generally drag it around with you wherever you go. If you attack it, you'll find that like Jason fighting the seven-headed hydra, when you lop off one head, another soon grows to replace it.

Glenda's Story

One of my Wounded Warriors--as I affectionately call my clients--is a woman named Glenda. Glenda's beast loves to eat. Much of her emotional support comes from eating. Genetically, Glenda is predisposed to be a larger person, but mentally she tortures herself with the desire to maintain a body style that is not truly her own. Because she "bought the Playboy standard" as the only way to be beautiful, she would feel miserably defeated when she didn't "measure up." Here the face of her beast was the rigid, unrealistic social standards created by her own mind.

Glenda's pattern was to eat whatever and as much as she wanted, and then go on a starvation diet to lose weight. After enough weight was lost and her ordeal was over, Glenda would resume eating in her usual pattern and blow up all over again, often gaining back more weight than she had lost while dieting.

Since body consciousness is like a wild animal, when it is restrained by force it rebels. For Glenda, this rebellion meant overeating and putting on more weight. During Glenda's many crash diets, survival issues and financial fears constantly plagued her mind. Her beast was only trying to survive what it feared was the next world famine. Her emotional storms were just natural mental responses to her beast's anguish over starvation. When we experience adversity, the body's survival programs are triggered--the beast reacts.

Diets do not work. Our bodies use the same strategy to build fat cells as they do to build muscles. Weight lifters build muscles by tearing down a portion of their muscle cells, which the body replaces and puts on a little extra to ensure that it will survive another such breakdown.

To permanently train our beast we must permanently modify its behavior. This takes patience, discipline, and mindfulness. Lasting change means a repeated effort firmly grounded and cultivated over a long time. The only trick that works is to stop crash dieting, to accept our body's style as a holy creation, and with a minimum effort, feed ourselves in healthy and loving ways and lose a maximum of a pound a week.

Glenda's weight problem was at one time her cross to bear. Through therapy and being moderately controlled, she learned to love herself and trust in the wisdom of her body to maintain its natural critical weight. When Glenda transcended her self-condemnation, her beast stopped betraying her, and now her weight stays in a moderate range with a minimum of effort. Her beast may always require a short leash, but in time, she may no longer need to control it. It will watch itself.

Dispelling Fear

Fear is a major face of the beast. Fear can exist as a worrying concern, a tension, or a weight that makes us feel timid. We only conquer fear by facing it and gaining control through "a courage borne of faith." If we are growing and developing, fear will be present. It is every Goddess Warrior's cross to bear. Fear always limits our choices. Only by taking small risks does fear drop away. Courage is fearing to do something but doing it anyway. Fear is like a grizzly bear. If we approach it when it's young, it can easily be tamed. But if we hide from it, it will continue to grow and eventually eat us. In other words, all that we repress increases. We need to watch that we don't feed our fears by avoiding people and situations that force us to confront them. If we are afraid of elevators and never go in one, that fear can grow into a full blown phobia.

Process fear by seeing and defining its boundaries. Put it in perspective. Most fears are paper dragons--negative fantasies that only appear real. Process your fear by using your creative imagination. Give it a good fight, for you really can control this inner drama. If you find yourself full of fear, go deeply into it and explore it thoroughly.

Close your eyes and breathe deeply and rhythmically. Turn toward your fear and ask if it is your ally or foe. Face it directly. Ask the fear to come into your consciousness. Where do you feel it in your body? Create an image of your fear. Give the image a voice. What does this fear want to say? Listen intently to this voice. It is an entrapped expression of your beast's beliefs. Talk to that side of yourself. Ask your fear what it has to teach you. If you find the fear to be a dark hole, a lead ball, a room made of big teeth, or a monster--go into it. Identify with it. Find a door to the image and step into it. Stand up to it and speak your mind. Find a way out of the dark hole. Put light on the lead ball. Find the spaces between the teeth or spray them with some magical disintegrating powder. Discover some creative way to transform your monster. Now move beyond it. Life will present you with repeated opportunities to face your fear.

You may avoid your beast for a while, but ultimately you will have to face it. You can learn to overcome fear by setting up situations that challenge it. Consciously try moving beyond your fearful limitations with skiing, whitewater rafting, mountain climbing, or skydiving. My colleague, Donna Atkinson, says, "Pushing through fear is far less frightening than the feeling of being powerless."

All transpersonal higher thoughts transcend the instincts of the beast. Trust in the Divine is the perfect antidote for fear. When you feel frightened, remind yourself that you made the fear up to feel more alive. Spiritually, your fear is a feeling of separation from the Goddess, which is an illusion.

Remember, Love is your source. The golden cord that connects you to Spirit is Love. Shine love forth to everyone and everything associated with your fear and then trust. Breathe deeply, come back to the present--and to love.

The Best Therapy of All

A young woman in the midst of tremendous emotional upheaval had an audience with a famous Tibetan yogi. For twenty minutes she poured out her heart to the master, telling him all the problems that were vexing her weary soul. She was hauling a heavy load and her beast, full of fear, was doubting her strength to survive the ordeal. The master patiently listened to her sad tale. Finally with tear-filled eyes, the young woman asked, "What can I do?" Whereupon the teacher looked at her compassionately and said in a soft but serious voice, "What you need, my dear, is to cultivate a good sense of humor," and burst out laughing.

It wasn't the answer she had expected, but in time she found that, like sunlight on ice, applying the warmth of humor to the knots of life, causes them to loosen and flow again. When Goddess Warriors ride upon their steeds of trust, armed with the gift of humor, they find that facing life's problems is no more serious than fighting toothless tigers.

All behavior consists of opposites. When we do anything over and over again, its polarity will arise. That is why it is important not to push too hard to make things happen.

Upon our Great Adventure, we stand between our highest and lowest nature. We live with one hand holding the golden cord of our celestial crane and the other tightly gripping the leash that restrains our beast. Balancing these opposites is the very essence of soulmaking. When we open to the totality of our being, in all its glory and depravity, we learn to direct our sensitivity, control our power, and live by higher, more universal, principles.

Balancing the Beast and the Higher Self

8

Balance Is Power

The Great Adventure is balancing the cosmic dance of shifting polarities. We unite our lower nature with our higher--the beast and the Goddess and blend our left-brain intellectual skills with our intuitive right-brain talents. This wedding fuses our male and female into a Worker of Light. To function in this world of conflicting realities, strive toward reaching a state of equilibrium. Remain poised in the space where opposing forces become equal partners.

Our male and female aspects fit together like inter-locking pieces of a puzzle. The Chinese sign of the Tao symbolizes this principle. Within the circle of the whole are two halves, and within each half lies buried the seed of the other. Carl Jung called a woman's inner male--the animus, and man's inner female--the anima. If we are to achieve completion, our male and female aspects must work together as a unified whole.

Two Sides of the Whole

Examine the female and male principles, not as roles but as two sides of a whole. The female force is yin, or implosive; the male is yang, or explosive. The female is the inner, receptive, magnetic side; the male is the outer, will-driven, dynamic side. The feminine is concerned with eros, interested in feelings and relationships. The masculine is logos, interested in the intellect and conquest. The female gives birth, creates space, and brings life to form. The male asserts, prods to action, and is out to win.

The female learns to be a partner of nature by connecting to its rhythms. The male is more prone to control and shape nature. The female can trust in the invisible and is willing to accept without naming. The male must name, categorize, and dissect. The female is growth oriented, the male is goal directed. She expresses as an unfolding, he speaks of facts.

It is female to surrender to the good of the whole, and male to "create your own reality." Visualize this difference by comparing a hunter with a fisherman. The hunter is the male counterpart, for he pursues and stalks his prey. The fisherman is female; after throwing out a baited hook, she waits patiently and lets nature take its course.

From the biological and sexual perspective, the female nature is slow to build, has great endurance, and is there for the long run. Inversely, the male is fast to build, sprints with full power, but lacks drive for the long haul. It is much the same as the difference between a weight lifter and a bricklayer. The weight lifter, the male counterpart, will press more than four hundred pounds in a single lift, but lifts it only three times. The bricklayer lifts only a few pounds at a time but lifts several tons per day.

Angeles Arrien summed it up when she said, "If you have a good relationship with words, deeds, power and exploring the meaning of things, you have a good relationship with your male. If you have a good relationship with vision, beauty, honoring the sacred, and organizing and structuring things, you have a good relationship with your female. For a man or woman to claim femininity, they have to overcome issues of pride and being special. To claim the male, issues of inertia and irresponsibility have to be overcome." Equalizing male and female energy is crucial to becoming whole, whether for an individual or society in general.

Balance Through the Personality

Mystic themes intersect our lives. Themes that, for thousands of years, were commonly thought to be reflected in our astrological charts. For me, astrology is an archetypical map, a rich language or nomenclature to describe human behavior.

Our personalities are made up of numerous tendencies, yearnings, inclinations, and potentials. Everyone has five personal directors. To illustrate, visualize the different subpersonalities by dividing them into a King and Queen, who represent the Sun and the Moon--our conscious and unconscious parts. The Princess and Prince within are Venus and Mars, our social aspects--our magnetic and dynamic sides, often seen as the give-and-take within our personalities.

In the following illustration the chalice represents Venus (the female symbol). She signifies our receiving nature. Fire illustrates Mars (the male symbol), since he embodies our drives and motivational natures. Mercury depicts our intellect, which informs and links them all together. The caduceus, our modern doctor's symbol, exemplifies Mercury who is androgynous.

The Sun and Moon plus Mars and Venus form two pairs of complementary opposites. The powers of Sun and Mars combine to form our male qualities, or animus. Part I. of this book (WAKE UP) covers the development of our male qualities, such as focus, will and assertion. The Moon and Venus, which form our anima, are discussed in Part III. (INVOKE THE GODDESS). The Moon represents our inner nature--our Goddess powers, whereas Venus is the erotic and creative nature--our womanly wonders.

Awakening female power is about balance. *Examine the illustration on the next page, then look within and see which side needs attention.* Instigate growth by increasing the elements needed for balance.

The Female Leads Individuation

Balance happens when we awaken our inner nature by focusing inside, listening to our bodies, feelings, and intuition. Then we transform these insights into action. Integration happens by living from the inside out, by aligning our internal with our external life. Jung called it "the process of individuation." He defined the journey as the awakening of the unconscious by the conscious mind to achieve a state of lasting completion. He believed that the

**Our Personality Directors or the Male
Female Within**

unconscious leads the way by means of some secret design. The unconscious mind wishes to become conscious but inadvertently rebels against revealing its secrets until they are extracted through effort.

The Sun and Moon symbolize our conscious and unconscious minds. They provide the keys needed to tread the path to wholeness. The birth of the mythological twins Artemis and Apollo show this solar/lunar interplay. Artemis, the lunar twin, was born first. She emerged from the womb quickly and was born fully developed. Immediately after birth she acted as midwife for her brother's birth, which followed after nine long days and nights of labor. Artemis personifies our instinctual, emotional impulses, which are naturally mature, since they serve the birth of consciousness. Apollo represents our solar nature, our individuality, which fully develops only after considerable time and effort, and always needs support from our reflective powers. A determined patience to follow the inner nature is required for full, conscious identity to develop.

The process of individuation requires that we intentionally surrender to the intuitive instead of continually reasoning what to do. The answers are inside us. Inner wisdom comes by trusting our intuitive, emotional faculties to lead the way, but they must be closely supported by reason and a willingness to take action. Know what you want and then act. The male needs to be right there to assert what the intuition reveals. Like breathing, the female becomes the source of inspiration whereas the male is the source of expiration. Balance is achieved when we bridge the gap and hear what creative inspiration is saying to logical understanding--in other words, when we act with the male following the female.

When the male leads, we are listening to the intellect and follow goals and deadlines, despite inner promptings or universal messages. It is not always wise to have strict time limits on our goals. I learned this lesson graphically in the fourth year of this writing process. My mind believed that my manuscript would soon be ready and asserted that belief by setting a publishing deadline. Immediately after I set the deadline, I felt compelled to write on a very emotional issue. Then the printer broke down and Walter could not help since he was swamped with his own work. The timing was wrong, but I didn't listen to the signs of the Goddess. Instead my male locked into achieving the goal and bolted onward. I pushed Walter to finish editing any-way, which caused conflict and unpleasantness. When our inner male acts without the guidance of the wise female, there is always drudgery and waste. This action did not result in power for me. Power comes from being in a state of equilibrium.

Balance also requires discrimination of feelings, which is achieved by cultivating nonattachment. Attachment caused by desire is the source of our pain. Nonattachment frees us from its control. Paradoxically, only by detaching ourselves from material desires can we safely reap nature's rewards. I have learned that we can't have whatever it might be we want, until we let it go.

This first publishing attempt taught me that I could completely detach from my creative child, whom I served so diligently for four years, and begin again. It was liberating to be free after desiring something so much. Without discrimination, we are pushed by desires and agendas and do not follow our true inner rhythms. Remember, balance is the chief ingredient we seek in becoming whole, for only then do we further the Great Work.

9

Undisturbed peace of mind is gained by being friendly to those who are happy, compassionate to the miserable, delight in the virtuous and indifferent toward evil.

Yoga Sutra of Patanjali

Being Centered and at Peace

If the universe compares to the womb of the Divine Mother and our Earth the body of the Goddess--then we are her Cosmic Children. Identify with your Divine Child to connect with all the loving female energy that surrounds you. It is in the womb of silence that we seek our center and feel her sweet embrace swirling around and through us. That joy which we feel is our natural state, all other emotional states are but distractions of that one unified state of balanced, peaceful awareness.

The trick is: How do we maintain a "unified state of balanced, peaceful awareness" when our world could best be described as "chaos in action"? The following metaphor will help you understand how to do it.

Imagine the universe as a vast ocean, swirling around a small island at its center. This ocean is a ceaseless, boundless, turbulent whirlpool of vital force, but on the island at its center, as in the eye of a hurricane, there is relative peace. This island, inhabited only by a band of monkeys, has a temple at its center, built around the altar of absolute peace.

In a mystical way, we are this island and everything we experience is really ourselves. The various elements of this metaphor, as well as their relationships to each other, all have symbolic meaning. Monkeys represent our many subpersonalities. Each potency has a style strikingly different from the others, yet coexists within the whole. These monkey-like identities could live peacefully, provided they could harness some of their boundless energies; but as a rule, they are rarely content for long with anything. Driven by boredom and desire, they wade out through the channels of our senses into the whirling vortex, attempting to experience pleasure and happiness in the world outside. This vortex, dripping with sweet desire, is very seductive.

As we begin to move out from center, the force of the vortex increases. The farther we go from shore, the faster and stronger the currents become. Life becomes more and more exciting. We become more active and energetic and feel more alive. The farther we wade in our quest for "life, liberty, and the pursuit of happiness," the stronger the emotional forces become. Whether the feelings are pleasure or pain, we feel more alive. If we stray too far from shore--overreach in our pursuit of pleasure or overvalue emotional intensity--we are most often swept away.

In your drive for continuing emotional release, how often do you overextend and create drama? Drama gives life its "juice." How could you ever live without it? Why would you want to? If you don't see how you could, it may be useful to remember that is what you once thought about riding roller coasters and attending all-night parties.

A client's story illustrates this metaphor on a personal level: Marilu came to me because she was a social wallflower and wanted to get out more. She believed her quietness was the reason she intensely disliked parties and public gatherings. The problem was that whenever she would plan a social event she would become excited about attending and project her vision of how she wished it would be. As the big day drew closer, her excitement would mount until something would shatter the perfection of her illusion. She would end up feeling discouraged and abused. Marilu's lesson was to learn to be present in the moment and to stop her mind from wading out into the vortex in anticipation of future happiness.

Life is a continual barrage of sensory input followed by emotional output. When we "live in the fast lane," it is easy to be swept away. How we love to become emo-

tionally involved with things. "E-motion is energy in motion" Feelings constantly flow through us, often causing us to act unconsciously and involuntarily. Feelings come in waves--fluid signals that the soul sends to guide and motivate us. They are the feedback system to who we are. Their function is to personalize us, and focus us in time and space.

Whatever your feelings, accept them without judgment. Do not ignore them, or they will intensify. The quicker you acknowledge your emotions, the faster they can change. Many people do not know what they feel. And, if you are one of these, start to acknowledge your

feelings by checking yourself occasionally. I feel_____. If
you find yourself adding the word "that," for example I
feel that_____, you are probably coming from your head.
What you want is feelings, not thoughts.

Give yourself what you need in the present, and stop
rehashing old stories and reliving melodramas long past.
Don't gold-plate your garbage or wallow in your feelings.
Muster your energy and move quickly through your emotions. Spin them off. Find appropriate methods of expression to deal with feelings in the moment, and most of all,
don't dump them onto others.

*A Goddess Warrior's secret is to live completely
in each moment, allowing feelings their
expression. "Let them flow--let them go."*

Experience emotions and then allow them to vanish
without a trace. That is part of what surrendering to the
universe means--letting life's emotional currents flow
through you but not become a part of you. In this way we
experience life's ups and downs, and listen to their messages, without getting caught on the roller coaster.

Keep your "Watcher" on duty and sound the alarm
when you feel yourself going into turbulent waters. If you
constantly strive for busy activity, you may find intensity
and adventure, but you may be masking your emotions.
Besides, you are risking being swept away by emotional
storms that zap your power and leave you depressed,
lethargic, ill, or in a state of complete emotional burnout.
If you discover yourself drowning in painful emotions that
frighten or discourage you, know they will pass. Stop
resisting, go within, and surrender to the flow.

*Christ's favorite greeting was
"Peace be with you."*

His message says: Live in the temple of joyful peace at
your center, not in the excess gaiety of your periphery. At
the core of our being, far from the excitement of the vortex, is where the Higher Self resides. For many, this quiet
place seems dull and uninteresting. There is no emotional
power to drive away the boredom. Seek the peaceful pleasures to recharge your life-force by spending prime time
on your "island of calm."

Flora's Story

Flora once described being centered as "a bird sitting perched, not pulling, not pushing, just waiting for the appropriate moment." This comment marked a major breakthrough for Flora, for she had been dissatisfied with her relationship and her work for years. She would often say that she wanted peace, but she felt disconnected from her quiet inner self, which gave her a gnawing sense of restlessness.

The catalyst for growth came when Flora's comfortable but uncommitted two-year relationship with Bob ended. In frustration and anger, she said she wanted the relationship to end, but after it happened, she fell into great fear and resistance and experienced tremendous pain.

Although she did not know it at the time, Flora's loss had opened her "sacred wound." The pain of her estrangement brought back powerful adolescent memories of when she was thirteen and her mother died. Shortly thereafter, her father brought home a mail-order bride, who became the "wicked step mother," making Flora feel like Cinderella--unloved, and unwanted. She had been a good student, but her grades dropped, and she finally ran away to live with a relative.

This early experience had dug a deep rut in Flora's emotional stream-bed, deep enough to be called a sacred wound. Her sad "little maiden" was still exerting tremendous power, often making her believe that relationships didn't work for her. As a result of all these early experiences, Flora thought she didn't want commitment. She defined Bob as a warm companion and thought she was satisfied with that. After she lost him, however, she discovered that what she really wanted was a closer, more intimate love. Up from the depths of her unconscious had come the whale of those old memories of her childhood loss and, like Jonah, she was swallowed into the belly of separation and pain.

Bob enjoyed his freedom and began seeing other women. That drove Flora wild. She would stay up until all hours, her mind racing, her imagination running uncontrollably. She even started driving by his house, spying on him. Whenever she would see a strange car parked in front, she would believe it belonged to another woman. As time went on she waded farther and farther out into her emotional vortex, where she experienced a profound depression caused by her obsession.

Flora, determined to move beyond her pain, committed to regular counseling to help clear her emotional body of obstructions. She quickly broke through her self-imposed barriers and overcame her addiction to melodrama. She said, "I started to see the light. Why was I letting myself go bonkers over this? It was just another event in my life." Within only a few weeks of seeking peace as a life-style, she had a major breakthrough. Flora finally surrendered to the Force, opened her Goddess eyes, and saw all the love being offered to her. Her "old" eyes, covered by a film of expectation, couldn't see love presented to her if it did not come in the exact form she expected. With her blinders removed, Flora knew she was learning to trust herself and she plucked up the courage to ask for what she really wanted.

Shortly after her breakthrough, Flora and Bob left on an Hawaiian vacation to see if they could "sort things out." When they returned, Flora spoke joyously about her progress. Her words were so profound that I took notes. She said she had finally learned to be centered and balanced. "I'm sitting, perched like a bird, waiting for the right inclination to come," she reported. "Only when the energy comes to me do I move with it. I trust in myself. I feel myself present in the moment and I act from it. I feel like I am gliding along, not trying to push the river upstream." About her relationship she said, "When the wind blows, then we can fly together."

The universe tested Flora shortly after this conversation. Her company relocated and she lost her job. She battled with fear a couple of times, but generally she stayed centered and chose to take it as an opportunity to find better employment. Flora said, "I am acting from good intentions and I am true to myself. I finally trust. I know a sign will come so I'm no longer afraid." It did, and she got another job.

Flora was learning to let go of control by surrendering to her feelings in the moment. However, in her determination not to react to them, she overreacted and started to withhold feelings. "Withholds" are not saying what you feel. "Expressing every little feeling to Bob would be damaging," Flora said, "So I would just pull my energy inward in the moment and it would all pass quickly." This practice proved hazardous, however, for over time these little repressions increased, and she was not ready for the rage that finally assaulted her. From this she learned the necessity of healthy expression in the moment. The object is to release without pushing or pulling, letting feelings flow.

There were withholds on Bob's side too. One day Flora found him with another woman. She finally acknowledged her heartfelt need for integrity and a deeper commitment, and she cut off the relationship. This time leaving him gave her a sense of freedom, for her sacred wound had healed. Besides, she knew how to find her temple of peace. Despite Flora's pain and attachment, she courageously said "No" to what she didn't want--a relationship without trust and commitment--and let go. When we surrender to the Divine impulse, there is no other way than to trust and let go. Only then do the answers come and the doors open to a more harmonious pathway of life.

Flora's separation lasted six months. Bob stayed in touch via her child, using various excuses. When they finally talked, he opened with love and told her how much he valued and appreciated her and wanted their relationship. He came back, but it was a completely new and different relationship. Flora had found her power. She was strong enough to know what she wanted and centered enough to express it. She first had to heal her past, define her heartfelt desires--and then be able to release them.

Flora eventually left Bob again. She found that after another year together he reverted back into his old patterns of dishonesty. Flora realized that Bob mirrored her past and, because she had grown and changed, she had to shed the old and be open to what came next. This time she was amazed at how quickly she could cut off the relationship and heal her attachment.

Nonattachment, the Way of the Tao

Flowing with the universe means allowing the Goddess force to move through you. Holding too tightly comes from giving away too much or not taking in enough. Flowing with the Goddess is like playing in a mystical dreamland.

Knowing clearly what you want, but being willing to let the her creative abundance take care of specifics.

In Flora's case, she found that she wanted a deep monogamous relationship, but was not attached to who provided it. It is like trying out for a part in a play without being attached to any specific outcome. Nonattachment frees us from any consuming desire, for we are willing to let go, if need be.

Desire is the essence of creation, a deep passion to do and be, but just like a kid in a candy store, desire needs supervision. Our cravings bind the soul. As we free ourselves from all those imaginary needs and wants--everything that is not a deep heart's desire--we finally calm the restlessness of our mind.

The Great Adventure is being one with the Tao, which literally means "the gate through which all things move." It is what Christians call a state of grace. Although the Tao implies the path of least resistance, it is often the most difficult path to follow, for it requires tuning into our inner resources and surrendering to the flow.

The challenge comes because there is always emotional attachment to anything familiar. Memories impress deep grooves in the riverbed of the mind. These memories, like ruts in a muddy road, make the ways of the past, rather than the present, our path of least resistance. The past is our greatest trap. Timothy Leary said, "You are only as young as the last time you completely changed your mind." Memories captivate the mind and wrap the ego in a warm blanket of status quo to form our belief systems, which often choke the natural flow of the universe. Change your belief systems and you change your frame of reference. Otherwise you will live life through a veil of emotional conditioning, seduced onto a treadmill of self-fulfilling prophecy.

To release limiting beliefs some of your monkey-like subpersonalities may need "reframing" or "reprogramming." I spent years doing affirmations, guided imagery, and hypnosis as techniques to change my programming. We are creators and need processes to work on changing our personal mythologies and awakening new sides of ourselves. These "create your own reality" practices taught me to take responsibility for my life and to manifest in the physical world. Ultimately though, the quest is always a co-creation with the Divine. Align first with the universal symphony and then express your innate creativity. Now, I just focus on the Divine, follow my joy, and do my work, letting my daily needs take care of themselves.

Too many people use spiritual practices to make material gains. It is often said, "Be careful what you ask for, because you might get it." How can we be absolutely positive that satisfying all our desires is for our highest good? For example, I know a man who magically created a 1.5 million dollar business within two years, only to have it fall into complete chaos--bankruptcy and litigation--two years later. In retrospect, I can see that not having great financial abundance in my early career was a spiritual blessing, for I might have become a spiritual yuppie, instead of a loving Goddess.

Take part in creation by being aware of your thoughts and beliefs, but do not strong-arm the universe. Creating form with tricks of magic continually diverts the River of Life. When we constantly swim upstream, we create waves of resistance. Continual redirection brings struggle, for whether we are pulling or pushing, our power diminishes by blocking the universal flow.

When we are constantly creating our own special reality, it is as if we are pushing the talk button of a two-way radio. We are broadcasting just fine, but all we hear is the sound of our own voice. To receive the universal message, it is necessary to take our fingers off the "send" button. Choose what you want, then surrender; otherwise, you won't hear the inner messages or awaken your female power.

Surrender into Being Centered

Surrender is a step toward peace and the dance within the harmony of the Tao. It is trusting in the divine order of the universe, and following life's currents. Surrender is the opposite of resistance. Resistance is trying to change people or conditions. It is a blocking motion that keeps our emotions in a state of perpetual excitement over issues based on fear and survival. Without resistance, we release the fight for control, and naturally flow with the force of the Tao. Often this means the death of who we *think* we are.

If you believe that the only reason things aren't worse than they are is that you are holding on for dear life, the thought of surrender is as frightening a dragon as you are ever likely to face. Surrendering to the process lets love guide the way. Yield to love, for it is the light of who you are. To awaken your spiritual nature, merge your emotions in an attitude of surrender. Tune all your feelings to a spiritual frequency--the energy of love and divine oneness. Choose to live, moment by moment, in a higher vibrational state.

Practicing Meditation

We are wise to purify our perceptual channels through quiet time. Take time each day to meditate. Remember the temple? It is a peaceful, quiet inner sanctuary, away from the warring factions outside. To find your Goddess, stop your outer activity and go inside your sacred space. Feel those divine impulses! The outer world is rich in activity, excitement, chaos, confusion, and stress. The inner world is quiet but rich in Spirit, imagination, tranquility, and joy. Learn to find nourishment in your Source and awaken inner vision.

When we meditate, we transform the material concerns of the beast into the spiritual essence of the Goddess. By practicing concentration, the monkey-mind gradually comes under control and confusion fades. Remember, concentrating on the task at hand makes life a meditation. When we conquer internal discord, we automatically flow with the breath of the Goddess in harmony with the eternal Tao.

Meditation is easy to learn. All you have to do is focus upon your highest purpose, be patient, and wait. It is any practice that leads to lasting control of the mind. One process is "letting the mind be"--being open, aware, and attuned. The mind then becomes a flow of energy, neither forced too tightly nor allowed to run loose. We bring our attention inward, beyond the limited realm of our senses, beyond fear, desire, and struggle. It may sound exotic and yogis may practice meditation for years to receive the fullest truth, but we can literally transform our lives with only a few minutes of meditation each day. This says a lot for the power of practice and repetition.

Find your temple through some kind of daily practice, so in peace you shall live.

Find you temple by sitting quietly for at least fifteen minutes a day. Make you body comfortable with your back and head straight and your spine aligned with gravity (head up). Sitting is best, for when you lie down to meditate, you are more likely to fall asleep.

Close your eyes and breathe in and out very evenly. Clear your mind of everything. If a thought or sense stimulus should intrude upon your peace, mentally shout "Stop!" Then watch. Listen. Bathe in the sound of silence. After a while your mind will become fatigued and thoughts will start to roll in fast. Just let them drift by. Be their shepherd. When thoughts arise, look at them, and then center your thoughts on the Goddess. Say, "I am Light, I am Love, I am Goddess," over and over again.

After you learn to shut off your thoughts, you will find your Watcher: a separate faculty at work--a mind within a mind. The nonverbal Watcher helps us stay focused, provided it is awake. Identify with your Watcher, for this powerful faculty can aid you in everything you do.

Success on the path comes quickly for those who are diligent and consistent. It may sound hard, but that is why it is called "the road less traveled." Yet it's as easy as dedicating a little time each day to self-improvement. My daily meditation ritual often includes breathing exercises, identification with the Goddess, staring at a candle, and reciting a mantra. It stabilizes me, helping me stay centered and balanced.

Finding peace comes naturally when we find our inner temple. Your inner temple my be a magical room made of crystal spheres, it could be a nature scene. Find any quiet sanctuary--an inner space--where you can be poised and centered in the Goddess.

"Poised" is being balanced or composed, a combination of peace and power. When you are poised and identified with the Goddess, you have the strength to do and the effectiveness to be. You move away from reaction and operate from your divine impulses within. Be the spirit of the Goddess. Merge with your Source by recognizing your Divine nature, an expression of wonderment and ecstasy. Invoke Shakti, the female force, by letting the light of Cosmic Motherhood and Universal Sisterhood shine in your heart. Peace is your natural state and divine right.

III. INVOKE THE GODDESS

10

*Our earth is ready to come of age
through you as the awakened,
enlightened, loving and powerful
Goddess.*

Terry Cole-Whittaker

Experience Being a Goddess

Being a Goddess means shining reverently and expressing your true feminine nature. The Sanskrit name for Goddess is *Devi*, which means "to shine with its own light." Being a Goddess means trusting in your spiritual connection.

If you want to *understand* the Goddess and absorb her powers, you can't just observe, you have to *stand under* and comprehend her. You need to grasp and be one with her and enter the consciousness of Divine Love personified. That is why "identification is the master key." The process is recognizing the Goddess qualities within yourself.

The secret to understanding the Goddess lies in learning Holy Theurgy, the art of becoming the god-form.

The Goddess inside is a yin place, a deep inner reservoir, a garden that reflects all creation. We become the Goddess when we are open and receptive, for she can only be truly known through direct experience.

The Transformative Love Force

The way of the Goddess is love. Love is accepting and empowering yourself and others to do and be your best.

Mother Theresa said, "As I love, no man can love. Women are the heart of the world." Love is sharing and works through interpersonal relationships. It links and unites, unlike the mind, which defines and separates. Love creates, sustains, motivates, and enhances.

Our love nature is alchemical--a powerful force that can change, transform, and regenerate life. In medieval Europe, the masses believed that alchemy was a physical process that could transmute lead into gold. To advanced practitioners, however, alchemy was an esoteric psychological study designed to transform the gross material nature of the alchemist into the golden radiance of holy wisdom. Love values and encourages human development. It is what makes transformation possible.

Be Compassionate

The soul of woman is compassion. To awaken female power, we must make compassion the first condition of our work. Campbell said, "Compassion is an awakening of the heart from bestial self-interest to humanity. It is a sympathetic emotion that connects and binds through love. It literally means to 'suffer with'." With compassion, we become Goddesses at our core and therein lies our transformation.

Living in the Heart of the Goddess

The Goddess embraces all spiritual force, and yet she is deeply grounded. The Great Goddess, the essence of female power, exists in all that is, animate and inanimate, for the universe exists within her womb. Her body is the solar system, the Earth, and the physical body within which we dwell. She is Mother Nature, whose seasons and cycles of natural evolution guide all life to fruition. Woman's magic is Earth magic. She births and sustains life, just as the Earth bears the plants that feed us.

The female side of God has virtually been ignored in the West, except for the Blessed Mother, who was the vechicle of the Christ. Christian teachings see God as the Holy Trinity--Father, Son, and Holy Ghost--which is thought to be all male. The Holy Spirit is really a feminine force, for it is the same wondrous power that is called "Shekinah" in Judaism and "Shakti" in Hinduism. God is

We are all one earth family.

My Mother Earth illustration shows how we are all interconnected and must bind together with love and compassion. Drawn without arms and legs, it shows how the planet is at the mercy of its people.

also Mother and Earth, and we all are expressions of the
One Mother/Father God.

Reviving Your Moist Creativity

The Goddess is the ceaseless creator and protector, a
consuming potency that compels us to expand ourselves
and produce new forms. She produces, preserves and lets
go. Marija Gimbutas, after researching the Goddess for
twenty years, said, "The main theme of the Goddess symbolism is the mystery of birth and death and self-renewal,
not only human but all life on earth and indeed in the
whole cosmos."

The Goddess is what Hildegard called "greening
power." Her term *viriditas* translates as "all creativity,"
or "God's freshness," which humans receive through their
life force. Like the regenerative power of spring, we too,
have this lush refreshment or vital ability to bear fruit.
Hildegard says the real sin is "drying up," in other words,
ignoring or losing our ability to create.

Female power is staying wet and moist; in essence, it
means staying a part of creation. Immediately after I read
The Illuminations of Hildegard of Bingen by Matthew
Fox, my life flooded with greening power. I started drawing
the many faces of the Goddess and, to my amazement, I
could create images rich in symbolism. I never thought I
could illustrate, yet a deep desire to create and a new
found ability to do so was awakened.

Awakening female power is a journey of self-expression
that happens by participating in life. Hildegard pulled herself from a sickbed to write her book; the process took ten
years. It was not the book that healed her but "the process of using art as meditation." Likewise, my process of
writing, drawing and teaching has awakened my female
power. It is the process of expressing and being creative
that awakens our greening power and heals us from
repressive psychological conditioning.

The Unifying Force

Metaphysically, the Goddess symbolizes the one unified
force from which everything is created and into which
everything returns. *Star Wars* called it, "The Force"--an

energy field created by all living things, surrounding, penetrating, and binding everything together. The Chinese call it, "The Tao," which is a study of the universe that explains why it works the way it does. Campbell said the Goddess encompasses all time and space. Terry Cole-Whittaker used the term, "Godus." The Goddess is all there is, and we are all One and in this together.

Eastern mythology sees the gods and goddesses as only existing in pairs, where the female operates as the actual to the male's potential. They believe that all power comes from the female. In the Hindu Shiva/Shakti polarity, Shiva technically does nothing. He represents the "unmoving infinite potential," which is a latent force that works only through his Shakti. Shakti (or whatever form in which the Goddess is worshiped) is the "infinite actual." The female does everything. She represents the energy of motion that powers an ever changing universe.

Celebrating the Goddess with Ritual

Glorify the Goddess with rituals and ceremony. Create a sacred place somewhere in your home, an altar to the Divine. The power of ritual is that it works with the unseen to create psychic and psychological changes within us. The practice of ritual affirms our divine connection, bridging our inner and outer worlds. The word "ceremony" comes from the Latin word that means sacredness. Campbell says, "Creating a ritual is an enactment of a myth, by participating in the rite, you participate in the myth."

See each person as divine, as a Goddess or God. The Hindus have a salutation of great reverence. This gesture is the universal symbol of prayer. Put your hands together in front of your heart with the fingers pointing upward, and bow to the divinity within. The greeting, "Namaste " (pronounced, "Na mast aye") loosely translates as "the Goddess within me greets the Goddess within you."

Our society seriously lacks meaningful rituals. There is an awkwardness and resistance to their creation. But remember, anything you do with consciousness will work. Your rituals can be spontaneous or planned. They can include personal daily tasks, such as dressing or eating; gestures, such as lighting a candle or tying a ribbon; or intense group ceremonies known as dramatic rituals. Eating a freshly baked apple pie can be a ritual honoring the nourishing goodness of motherhood. Be creative. As you evolve, you will discover what fits your individuality.

When you are a Goddess, all life becomes sacred.

Real power comes when we arouse our devotion and apply our will to go deep inside, for what we ultimately seek is Unity with the Absolute. Devotion is the power that makes identification possible. Called "*bhakti*" in Sanskrit, this blissful altered state is the highest form of love, for even a little will profoundly open the heart center. All you need to do is meditate, pray, chant, sing litanies, or focus on an image or photograph and you will awaken bhakti. This reverence comes by offering dedication to your "*Ishta Devata*," your chosen ideal, whether it is the Blessed Mother, Christ or Buddha. My chosen ideal is the Divine Mother, and she takes the form of the Earth--one Earth, One Family, and One Source.

Being empowered by the Goddess accelerates the process toward wholeness and creates great change. When we gain direct knowledge of the Goddess, divine love awakens within our hearts and we experience our womanly wonders. We merge in the cosmic play and awaken our Shakti, the energizing force of creation. Every day changes into a ritualistic dance of joyous transformation.

11

Goddesses that Live Within

The Goddess Force exists outside us, forming an invisible thread of support with which we can identify. All the different archetypical goddesses are the semblance of the Great Goddess image. Known as the Giver of Bliss, she has many names, like Kali, Shakti, Prakriti and so on. Her forms are endless, although She is One.

In the following chapters, I introduce some important goddesses who live within each of us. As you read, let the stories absorb your imagination until you feel the archetypes manifest within. Be an actress and step into the different roles. All you have to do is embody the Goddess for a time and you will receive her powers.

This sampling of mythical archetypes will help you through the "We Are" phase of the quest. Each goddess is a part of our collective heritage. Each offers an understanding of our inner psychological drives, and gives us invisible support so we can get the help we need.

In the *personality* the feminine psyche is seen through the Moon (our inner resources or Goddess powers) and Venus (our magnetic nature or womanly wonders).

The Greek archetypical goddesses are experienced through the three *types* of goddesses--virgin, vulnerable and alchemical. The Virgin is independent and self-contained, like Hestia, Athena, and Artemis. Vulnerable goddesses are dependent and cover the traditional roles of child, maiden, mother and wife. The stories of Persephone, Demeter, and Psyche offer wisdom to women who link and receive their fulfillment through others. Aphrodite is the primary Alchemical Goddess.

We will identify with some goddesses more strongly than others, which can be either a bane or a blessing, but with practice we can gain access to all. By tapping into the powers of love, we all can live alchemically and transform our lives.

Shine sometimes as an Alchemical Goddess, sometimes as a Virgin Goddess, sometimes as a Traditional Goddess, for through them you open to the powers of the Great Goddess. Awaken the Divine Goddess by allowing her many faces to encircle you.

Embodying the Goddess Kali

As Goddess Warriors living in the age of Kali, let us learn to invoke her image. She transcends personality and holds the keys of transformation. As the Hindu story goes:

Brutal male demonic forces dominated and oppressed the world for a long time. These dark powers had received the boon of invincibility from any man. Even the most powerful deities were suffering defeats. None could do anything to stop the deadlock so, in desperation, they prayed to the Divine Mother for help. The Great Goddess told the gods to join forces and combine their energies. Then they all concentrated upon a stream of fire that produced a brilliant supernova. Out of this light came the Great Goddess in the form of Durga. Kali sprang forth from the brow of Durga and filled the skies with a roar. Together they fought a battle that destroyed demonic oppression and restored peace and balance to the world.

Kali's myth shows how, in a deadlocked situation, the female is the only moving element. The Goddess must emerge to break male dominance. She serves as the Guardian who protects the treasure and summons a powerful voice to show us the way.

Some of Kali's faces are gracious, some are cruel, some are loving, some are destructive, but all are part of life. Although Kali's wrathful side is fearful, she shows us the need to destroy the false attachments that hinder our spiritual growth. Kali's fight is an inner war. Her mission is to destroy all that blocks truth. Her omnipotent forces wipe out the ego-centeredness that keeps us off balance.

Kali carries a severed head, suggesting the destruction of our untruthful and limiting selves. Something must be eliminated or rejected in order to have new life. *What do you need to let go of in your life?* Be willing to release anything that is no longer needed, anything that prevents you from achieving a more universal consciousness. Let go of something, even if it means starting small by cleaning out your closet.

What are those less conscious emotional needs and habit patterns that you have carried over from your past to manifest when you least expect it as compulsions and obsessions? Search for those old ego structures, attitudes, physical addictions, or safety/security attachments that block your usable power. We discover these unconscious patterns in our relationships when they become battlefields. Here as in all cases, victory comes by conquering the self.

To uncover your inner darkness (a pattern that needs to be cast out), become like the Goddess and go beyond the ego. When you feel a pain, listen to it, emphasize it, mourn it, recognize the grief, but do not judge, rationalize, or try to change it. By genuinely accepting a quality or pattern, paradoxically, it changes.

Kali wears a necklace of severed heads and a girdle of human arms. Her garland of heads represents her treasury of knowledge and wisdom. Originally there were 52 heads, each representing a character of the Sanskrit alphabet, believed to form the basis of all knowledge. Coincidentally my illustration of Kali has 26 heads, which forms our alphabet. Kali's message is: seek knowledge and let go of attachment. Her skirt of severed arms illustrates the uselessness of all our grasping, "'I want and I own," which either puts us into the fear of not getting enough or the fear of losing what we have.

You may be called to sacrifice a cherished part of yourself, usually a personality trait, which can feel like emotional loss. A wise soul learns to face that cross with tranquility, knowing that out of the ashes of the past, new life is born. Change is inevitable, so surrender to the Goddess and let go of resistance. Resistance brings increased inner pressure. What you resist, persists.

Kali symbolism holds our answer. She sprang forth from Durga, whose name means "Beyond Reach." This tells us Durga was not dependent on another, and we too, should be one unto ourselves. They joined forces to eliminated the dark forces and there was peace.

Kali is a three-eyed goddess, which implies the power of our inner vision, which covers the past, present, and future. Her upper right hand holds the sword of discrimination, and the two remaining hands dispel fear and encourage spiritual strength. Her protruding tongue symbolizes the need for expression and participation in the world.

For me Kali is a Force, an intensity to shatter all obstacles. I feel this Goddess as an impulse, a knowing, an opportunity, and a wisdom. Bit by bit, she is built inside. My message from Kali is to go beyond the personality, the lists, the archetypical models which have created walls and mirrors. Sever all the heads--ego trips. Release all attachments to "who I am," "what I know," and "where I am going." Accept that I am a multi-dimensional being, a Goddess of Divine impulse with presence in every moment. Oddly enough my lesson in letting go started with becoming totally aware of myself and my environment in each moment. I must eliminate relating as the child or mother, but become conscious, and relate as a loving woman with presence.

Before you tear down all the mirrored walls, let go any limiting personal beliefs and experience the archetypical models. Look into the many faces of this Divine Oneness, try them on, and find parts of yourself. Then "let go and let the Goddess."

Hestia, the Keeper of the Sacred Fire

Hestia, the Virgin **Goddess of the Hearth**, is the least known of the major Greek goddesses, but she is the most essential to awakening our female powers. Known as **Vesta** to the Romans, she represented the living flame, central to the home and hearth. "Hearth" in Latin means

Kali's Sybolism Is the Key to Change

"focus." Hestia is symbolic of the "journey homeward or the return to oneself." The Goddess and the fire are one. She is the illumination of that spiritual fire at our center that unifies us. In ritual, she signifies the consecrated fire of home and temple. Honored in all temples of the Old World, she made all places holy. Her symbol is a circle, the sign of wholeness. She represents the eternal Light, which comes from being still and focusing inward.

Hestia is the key to being centered and balanced. As an inner reference point she allows us to be grounded in the midst of the confusion of the universal vortex. Hestia's gift of perception is the intuition gained by extended concentration upon the world that lies deep within.

Hestia Awakens Spiritual Centeredness

When you become Hestia you operate from a centered space, with an inner presence and a strong spiritual nature, objective and detached from any outcome. Hestia is not concerned with others and tends to withdraw into herself, seeking solitude. Invoke Hestia to bring deeper meaning into your life. With her, keeping house becomes an act of fulfillment rather than another tiresome chore. Dinner becomes a ritual, raising children an act of worship.

Hestia is a potent Goddess power that many of us neglect. Her force has expanded in my personality, for I feel more and more content to be alone, working upon something with meaningful purpose. She is the part of me

I named Sophia. I converted a part of my office into an altar, and every morning I am Hestia as I invoke the Goddess with ritual fire and incense.

If you have the Hestia archetype strongly placed in your personality, you have a self-contained nature that draws you to focus on the Divine. If not, I suggest you awaken Hestia to help your spiritual liberation. Let her bring you the peaceful order that comes from "contemplative housekeeping." Take time to focus and patiently absorb yourself in each task. Awaken her by concentrating on each moment. And remember: by simply lighting a candle or reciting a mantra, you can make even the simplest act a sacred ritual.

Athena, the Warrior Goddess

Athena is the Greek **Goddess of Wisdom and Craft**. Called **Minerva** by the Romans, she is often depicted wearing golden armor and carrying an owl. She was both Warrior Goddess and the protector of civilized life, home, handicrafts, and agriculture. She had a dramatic birth. She sprang fully grown, dressed in full armor, from Zeus' head. All the other god/ess bowed to her.

Also a Virgin goddess, she was committed to being "one unto herself." She was her father's daughter, Zeus' favorite child, and a self-righteous defender of the patriarchy. Zeus trusted only Athena to carry his weapons. Offering fortitude to the soldiers and many heros, Athena's martial and domestic skills planned strategy and executed purposeful thinking.

The Greeks credited Athena: with inventing the bridle to tame horses for humanity's use, with inspiring ship building, and with teaching people how to use the plow. She is that part of us that has practical wisdom.

The Athena archetype embodies the male qualities of logos. She uses intellect and will over instinct and nature, making her comfortable with men. To some extent she exists within us all. Cultivate Athena by educating your mind. Seek knowledge. Awaken her to receive her powers of clear intellect and diplomacy. As a symbol of the solar consciousness of women, she represents clarity through wisdom, reason, and purity. We embody the Athenian ideal by living in moderation--within the Golden Mean.

Athena Empowers Practical Wisdom

As I write, I am amazed at how much I identify with Athena. I, too, am a Goddess Warrior, and my writings have become a strategy for walking the Hero's Path. Athena is that part of me that intends to make something of myself and I am doing it with the help of a powerful man. Through the pursuit of wisdom and the development of my mind, I have grown into a patient and self-contained Athena.

Each archetypical goddesses has special boons to offer her devotees. To understand the richness of your inner nature, let's explore the Goddess powers of the Moon.

12

Moon as Our Goddess Powers

In the personality, the Moon is the key to our infinite inner potential. She is our Goddess powers. As an intimate ally, and **Self-Lover, Caretaker,** and **Image Maker,** she signifies the private, personal self, who informs us about how safe we feel in the world. She is our receptive nature--the answer to our deepest emotional needs. Our Moon is our path of least resistance. She comes out when we are in solitude, when we are reliving the past or are with our families, or when we are sharing feelings in intimate relationships. She is there when we eat, when we cry, when we dream, and when we care for ourselves and others.

Every person embodies several aspects of the Moon. Her face shines through the veneer of our personalities as **Child, Maiden, Mother, Madonna,** and **Wise Old Crone**.

The Greeks have the same word (*menos*) for both Moon and power. To be moonstruck meant to be chosen by the Goddess, blessed with gifts of woman. We can identify with any one of her talents: **Midwife, Sorceress, Light Bearer, Priestess,** and **Dreamer** by seeking tranquility and quiet introspection.

As an aspect of right-brain consciousness, the Moon operates through our subconscious motivations and intuitive insights. Her eyes glimpse the distilled essence of all

our past--feelings, thoughts, memories, impulses and con-
ditionings--those unseen influences that affect our daily
behavior yet lie beneath our levels of awareness.

The Fertile Sorceress and Midwife

Moon embodies the unseen, fertile, creative powers of
nature. We bind to our Moon, when we are connected to
our instincts, the earth, organic growth, and our ancestral
culture.

The Egyptian Goddess of the Moon was called **Isis**,
the wife and sister of Osiris, who was the God of Rebirth.
Egyptian Hermetics saw Isis as the **Great Symbol of
Female Power** and **Mother of the Universe**. They felt she
was the source of magic and sorcery. When Osiris was
dismembered by their brother Set, she relentlessly searched for his precious fragments. She found all but the phallus, which was devoured by the greedy crabs of the Nile.
The crabs are the symbol of those needy emotional drives
that, when left unattended, consume our ability to
generate new life.

Isis' restorative powers pieced Osiris together and re-
vived his body. With the use of an appropriate prosthesis,
she gave birth to Horus, the Sun God. Isis personifies
fertility, symbolized by the annual flooding of the Nile.
Moon has the light to make us pregnant and moist. She
embodies all womanly regenerative powers--the ability to
bear and raise children.

The Moon acts as a midwife in the birth of the Higher
Self and creatively aids in the purification and integration
of our many splintered subselves into a healthy unified
personality. I would suggest calling a Board of Directors'
meeting to confront your different subpersonalities, and to
persuade that mob to work together as a team.

The Moon teaches us to let feelings flow and find a
source of inner support. You find the Goddess within by
following your inner impulses and resources. Only then
will you know what is right for you in every moment.

Can you find your seasons and cycles, the ever-changing flow of creation and destruction? Ask: *Where am I on
my inner cycle? Am I birthing, generating or letting
go?*.

Artemis, Maiden of Internal Riches

In Greek mythology, Artemis was the **Goddess of the Moon and the Hunt**. Seen as a **Light Bearer**, she was in her element roaming the wilderness in the dark of night. Artemis followed her own inclinations. She stayed in the forest with a band of women and avoided the cities. Her policy was to be free from men and their influence. Also a Virgin goddess, she was the independent spirit who belonged to no man.

You are Artemis when you focus in your pure essence, uninfluenced by others. She is that part of us that is intact, competent, and self-assured; that part that can concentrate intensely to achieve a given goal.

I am Artemis in my work, for like her, my path is nontraditional. I go it alone. I separated from the masculine world of business to do what mattered to me. I roamed the uncharted wilderness of my own unconscious, and learned to see in moonlight, where details are muted and less distinct. I found psychic "techniques" to provide the light needed for inner vision. I have been Artemis in my relationships with women. In my past, there was always a changing band of women friends. Now, my sis-terhood is spreading through this book.

You too can easily learn to be Artemis, for everything you need to know is inside you. Everything you search for, like happiness, security, warmth, pleasure, and love, can be found within yourself. Yet most people believe happiness lies in the world outside. Our educational system and their effort to create a standardized, predictable world is largely to blame. These imposed structures put on our minds help us perform in today's corporate society but inhibit the development of our individual uniqueness, a view that is essential for creativity.

Feelings of unworthiness arise when we always look outside ourselves. Consequently, by not appreciating ourselves we learn to feel empty, restless, and incomplete.

As we merge in the light of our Lunar Goddess, we tap into the hand that rocks the cradle of our inner knowing, for she holds within her a treasure house of resources.

Linking With the High Priestess

We are all naturally psychic. We telepathically communicate with each other, whether or not we are aware of it. Everyone's female nature has a sensitivity capable of perceiving visual and mental imagery. Intuitive perceptions do not always come as prophetic visions. More often they are only a sense, a feeling, a movement, or a physical sensation.

To invoke your inner wisdom, identify with the High Priestess. Through intuition she whispers secrets in your inner ear. She links us with universal knowledge, the doorway to the unconscious. When we are the Priestess, our role is to withdraw from outer involvement and listen to the sound of silence. Only in silence can we find that quiet place inside where all answers lie: our special place of infinite knowing. There the voice of our soul speaks without words so that we may hear without sound.

I became a Priestess with the help of tarot and astrology. These symbols gave me a storehouse of internal images, which dissolved the gross distinctions created by my mind. They became a mirror for viewing the archetypal dance, which helped to improve my memory. Meditating upon the tarot symbols, especially the major arcana, reveals a rich hidden wisdom that cannot always be expressed in rational terms.

To awaken your intuitive resources, start by consciously opening your inner eyes. Tune into your feelings moment by moment to deepen and expand your perceptions. Relax and let the subtle intangibles lead you into psychic dimensions of awareness. Your inner resources are a true guide and asset, but to trust and decipher the Moon's messages, you need to be intimate with her. Her world is slippery and illusory. In moonlight you often see what is not there or mistake what is really there for something that is not. To accurately translate your insights into right knowledge, you must arm yourself with the two-edged sword of discrimination and learn to distinguish between illusion and reality.

You lose your ability to listen in an atmosphere of judgment and preprogrammed agendas. Judgment always spawns restriction and denial. To *receive,* you must free your intuition by controlling the ceaseless activity of your

**Silence is the Doorway to the
Unconscious**

mind. To *understand,* you must decorate your insights with the symbols of your intellect. And to *know*, you must realize with the whole of your being: body, mind and heart. Go beyond the facts, clear your mind and merge with your inner nature. Trust yourself to hear and just listen.

No matter what you perceive, it must be compared with your internal models for verification. If your intuitive faculty entwines with your desires, your vision will be colored. To know if an intuition is right, examine yourself. See if fear or desire drive you. Strong concerns distort your ability to see clearly. Look with your feelings and you will have an inner knowing. But to do so, you must let go of expectations.

If you do not understand, ask your Goddess for insight and be open to receive. Your questions will always be answered. But be forewarned: If you ignore the subtler answers provided by quiet insight, you'll get your messages through your body, environment, car, radio, TV, relationships, and especially with children. If you refuse to listen to the whispers, the universe will invoke your attention with a nudge. If you continue to ignore its subtler signs, "a bigger hammer" will be found. By awakening the Goddess, you will inherit the full wealth of her powers and be able to "see" where others find only darkness.

Merging With the Wise Old Crone

The Goddess shines through everyone as the Wise Old Crone. It is she who crosses the crossroads of consciousness--those places where ego surrenders to a higher will. The Wise Crone comes in solitude, in sleep, and near death--magical times where we reflect our truth. Her crazy wisdom and all-seeing eye enable her to view the past, the present, and the future in every moment. As the companion of our dreams and visions, the Crone converses with Spirit and works through enchantment, divination, and healing.

There are many wise Crones in this human potential movement, people and systems that are "helpers" with the process. I have found the Crone's knowledge through astrology, tarot, the *I Ching,* and Ralph Blum's *Runes.* I have found her healing through the bodywork I receive.

In ancient Greece the Goddess of the Dark Moon was **Hecate,** the archetypical Old Crone. Hecate, thought to be older than the patriarchal Zeus, was both feared and revered as the guardian of the underworld and the crossroads. Her gift was the ability to see within the blackness of the unconscious mind. She escorts us through the shadowy mysteries of life, and, just as Isis did for Osiris, she reunites us with our lost parts.

She gives us the strength needed to face our darkest truths. Hecate shows us what we are doing to ourselves and summons us to form an alliance with all our subpersonalities. Although this Goddess brings both ecstasy and madness, we need not fear, for when we invoke this Wise One within, she will attune us to our naked truth and guide us safely out of darkness and into the light.

Dreaming the Dream

We spend a third of our lives sleeping. Dreams are a magical celestial intercom with the Goddess. They are the doorway to unlocking unconscious treasures. Ask the Goddess for dreams that are inspirational, prophetic, or problem solving. She visits me every night in my rich and lucid dream world.

In Greek mythology, **Selene** represented the Moon itself. She loved only Endymoin, who was granted immortality and eternal youth, on the condition that he remain eternally asleep. Every night on broad wings, Selene clothed herself in the body of the Moon and rode across the sky, her brilliant crown illuminating mortals with dreams while she communed with her sleeping lover.

Scientific research has shown that everyone dreams six or more times every night, and the less soundly we sleep, the more likely we will recall dreams.

To remember your dreams, affirm them before falling asleep: I am remembering my dreams. Conscious mind, you will remember an important dream. Unconscious mind, show me your inner depths through clear symbols. Goddess, release my day and let this sleep be healing and regenerating as if I rest in your Divine arms. Let me see your wisdom so I can learn my challenges quickly.

Place a notebook and a pen or tape recorder near your bed, and record your dreams, as well as the feelings that were evoked. Logic and reasoning can interfere with understanding dreams. Always tune into the message of your emotions but do not attach yourself to the feelings.

It is best to awaken naturally. When you do awaken, let your first thoughts direct your mind back into its nocturnal exploits. Relive your dreams. Stay in bed an extra fifteen minutes to remember them. Using a dream journal is a valuable training exercise, for it provides the mental "gear" necessary to grasp and encode archetypal experiences symbolically.

Dreams are multidimensional, existing beyond boundaries of space and time. There, the past, present, and future occur simultaneously. The soul's messages are encoded in a complex symbolic language. Everyone has unique meanings for some symbols, while certain archetypical symbols are connected with all humanity. Dream books can be misleading, because the meaning of your images may differ radically from what they mean to others. Your best source for understanding your dream symbols is word associations.

According to Jung, when you use your dreams as a therapeutic tool, you are everything in the dream. Interpret your dream characters as sides of your inner nature.

To get more from the images, turn your dreams into meditations. Breathe deeply and identify with each symbol. Become it, then ask yourself: How do I feel? What do I want? Is there anything lacking? Do I have any reservations? To help you understand, embellish your dreams. Make them into a story, a ritual with sketches and a title. Use your imagination. They are your dreams and you can change the endings and may even choose to dream them again. Read Robert Johnson's book, *Inner Work* , for further study.

Take your conscious life into your dreams. Before you go to sleep, choose what you want to dream. Program what you want to learn. You can work out your issues, release pent-up emotions and test yourself for ethical perfection.

Ultimately our purpose is to become conscious when dreaming by spanning the boundary between waking and sleeping. Try lucid dreaming, which means having an awareness of who you are while you are dreaming. Next time you are dreaming, remember that you are dreaming and make a choice to do what you want.

As you awaken the Goddess within your dream world, you see that normal waking consciousness is, in essence, only another form of dreaming. So dream on.

Become the Great Madonna with the crescent symbol, for she contains the life of the soul. Trust your inner Mother to mirror the creative tides of your universe. Memorize her litany and say it daily to invoke your Goddess powers:

I am the Great Goddess,

Priestess of the Inner World,

I embody the sacredness of Motherpeace

Nurturing the outer world.

My way is to feel with the heart,

And find my own internal support.

In my dark world, beyond boundaries,

I hear the whispers of the universe.

I see my connection to all nature

And yet know that I am one unto myself.

The Goddess combines the need for joining with the knowledge that we are one unto ourselves. To truly acquire all the Moon's graces, you need to free yourself from attachment to past emotions that still bind you. You heal your obsessions and addictions by restructuring destructive emotional patterns. The process becomes just a matter of learning to love your Inner Child, a very "doable deed."

Awaken Your Moon and Access Your
Goddess Powers

13

Healing the Inner Child

Christian teachings say that we cannot pass into the Kingdom of Heaven unless we become like children. The Inner Child is our delightfully spontaneous side, where our dreams, wonderment and curiosity live. You would think with such a recommendation the wisdom of children might be listened to, but in society, children are generally not respected.

Everyone we have ever been is still a living part of us. Like rings in a tree, we just keep building new layers on top of our old personalities. Scratch the surface and what we find inside is an infant, a child of four, a five-year-old, a six-year-old, and so on. Knowing, loving, and raising this mob is the key to healing our unconscious natures and to discovering what our real needs and desires are. Every seeker must become responsible for her or his Inner Child. This little person is always there no matter what our age and needs unconditional love and acceptance.

A cousin shared a frightening dream. She wanted my feedback, because a good friend of hers had a similar dream at about the same time. In her dream she had another baby, but this child was wasting away and she felt helpless to do anything. I asked her if she was in touch with her own little child within, and she said, "No." Many women forget the child within when they become mothers or when they work in the world. Through lack of attention, the child withers away, bringing a dullness that stems from a lack of joy.

Usually that part of us that we try to avoid is the angry, fearful, possessive, jealous, sullen monster who lives within. A hungry Inner Child acts in needy ways because it is necessary for its survival. But if we ignore the child, it won't go away, it will eventually explode into an emotional outburst.

For years I ignored my Inner Child, yet a predominately childlike nature colored my persona. I looked outside myself for my completion, and found only what I lacked. My attachments dragged me through some uncomfortable places. During one period of my life, my Needy Nelly rebelled and obsessively demanded my full attention. She healed only after I awakened my Inner Mother to be there for her. I resolved the neediness of the child, who fed on dependency, by filling those empty spaces within myself. Honor your own Inner Child and be your own Caretaker. Start letting yourself be enough.

Activating the Inner Mother

Your child may control you through manipulation, depression, sickness, or by making you drink or eat too much. Call upon your Inner Mother to be there for you. Let her overcome any deficiencies. Commit to loving yourself unconditionally.

My own story is a vivid example of how miraculously this can work. My Needy Nelly was a problem child. She feared there wasn't enough for her and that she would never get what she wanted. So for two and a half months I consciously acted as if I had a child. I created an altar in my room and placed a decorated childhood doll upon it. I became the loving, supportive Mother who constantly told my Inner Child, "You can have what you want. You deserve it." I framed pictures of myself, both as a baby and as a little girl. I talked to them daily and even took them places. Each night I would go to sleep holding a teddy bear named Nelly. I would surround her with love and affection as I drifted off. At other times when uncomfortable feelings came up, I disassociated from them, acknowledged that they were only Nelly's cry for attention, and continued to be the loving parent. This process changed my energy from needy and uncomfortable to nurturing and loving.

We attract people who mirror our own beliefs about ourselves, and I was tired of meeting men who reflected the belief that I couldn't get what I wanted. With Nelly healed, the door opened and I found that I could trust and love again. I attracted a loving mate who gives me more than I ever expected. Finally, there is enough!

Once, a client came to me in a state of deep depression. She was afraid of facing financial ruin, anxious visions about losing her home and having her possessions auctioned off filled her mind. I took her on a guided imagery and together we separated the all-consuming fear of her timid little girl from the steadfast courage of her Divine Mother. From then on, whenever worry entered her mind, she would identify with her Inner Mother and nurture her Inner Child. Through this simple process she transformed her fear into constructive support and faced her dilemma squarely. With a stronger hand on the helm she was able to see her problems as they were and not as she fearfully imagined them to be. Like all "bogey-men," her fears were bigger than life. She didn't lose her house or her possessions, but she did learn an important lesson: she could be her own strength and her own helper.

Create an inner drama by imagining yourself nurturing and caring for your little child. To find your Inner Child, close your eyes and breathe deeply and rhythmically. Then assume there is a small tap at the door. Ask the "little you" to come in and, with the eyes of your imagination, see how old this child is. If you find that imagery is difficult, make it up verbally. Give your little child a nickname--any name other than your own (it helps to differentiate your child subpersonality from your conscious self). Then ask your Inner Child what she/he needs. Listen, love, and then take responsibility to fulfill your child's needs. Cherish your child, for there you awaken your spark of wonderment and joy.

Feeding your Inner Child is a powerful and practical way to transform emotional problems, for you learn to detach from feelings without denying them. In essence you change nonproductive feelings through cultivating unconditional love. You reprogram your childhood and create a new personal myth. When your child is healed, you break the unconscious bonds created by family and genetic programming.

Moving Beyond Genetic Programming

Genetic programming is important in understanding human behavior and releasing the past. An article entitled "The Eerie World of Reunited Twins" (Discover, 9/87) revealed recent discoveries explaining genetic programming. For over eight years a research team at the University of Minnesota, headed by psychologist Thomas Bouchard, tested a random sampling of 77 sets of twins and 4 sets of triplets separated at birth. Each set was rigorously tested for more than six days. The results of these tests produced some fascinating disclosures.

Character traits are more determined by genes than by environment. One example of twins separated at birth found that they not only had the same face and body, but also the same mustache, sideburns, and the same glasses. They were both firemen, "drank the same brand of beer, and held the bottle with the little finger stretched awkwardly beneath the bottom. Both were bachelors who were compulsive flirts and raucously good humored." Another set of twins discovered after they were reunited that "they smoked the same cigarettes, drove the same make of car, and had the same type of job."

What this verifies about human beings is the nature of the beast. Our inherited DNA programs us with a powerful set of behavioral instructions. These patterns are a part of our brain's hardware, that was given to us by our biological parents. Most of us do not have a twin acting as a "behavioral mirror" in which to compare ourselves, but our genetic code determines the make-up of our personality just as much.

Parental Forgiveness

Until we overcome the "baggage" we inherited from our parents and siblings, we continually act out their unconscious scripts in our relationships with others. Over and over we play out the same tired old parts with our friends and lovers in a futile attempt to heal prior family business. My first live-in relationship was my mother's astrological twin. We create and attract that to which we are accustomed, for unconsciously we seek familiarity, not necessarily happiness. Our relationship with our families serves to exemplify those parts of ourselves that need to be healed. They give us something needed for our evolutionary growth.

As we forgive our mothers and fathers for not being perfect parents, we transcend the attachment and heal ourselves. See your parents as real people. Strip away the parental roles. The key to personal liberation is allowing your parents to see things their way. Stop seeking their approval; instead, provide it. Change your perspective by giving love rather than expecting to receive it.

Through the therapeutic process of going back into the past and relating to your parents, you can release unexpressed feelings. Imagine how you wished your childhood had been. By recreating childhood interactions, you can gain insight into your parents' own emotional needs. Once during therapy I visualized my mother's emotional consciousness while I was young. I saw where I inherited my feelings of "never enough." Realizing that it was her pattern, not mine, gave me a new sense of freedom. I could let go of that tendency to be fearful and cautious and was more able to joyously express my true self.

One day my client, Betty, broke down and cried. A male friend had screamed at her in a way that mirrored how her father had treated her. At first Betty wanted to blame her friend and direct her pain back at him, but she quickly acknowledged him as just an emotional trigger for the long-standing issue with her father. In session, she visualized her father standing before her and spoke openly with him. The session ended when she was full of heartfelt forgiveness. The next day Betty called, saying she had just received a check from her father for a thousand dollars. This synchronicity was a tangible sign that she had healed her past emotional scars.

Call or write your parents as a gesture of appreciation. It is even possible to heal a relationship with those who have died. By truly loving your physical parents whether dead or alive, you become closer to the Divine Mother and Father. Unconditionally loving your parents is the first step to understanding these heavenly beings. If you resist your natural parents, you block the divine forces they represent. The Chinese understood this principle, for elaborate rituals were performed to propitiate the ancestors who were believed to be a link to heaven.

As you forgive your parents, your children will forgive you. And as you heal the Inner Child and acknowledge the Inner Parent, you are free to move beyond genetic programming and release the hold of the past.

14

Exploring the Maiden's Journey

The Maiden is the budding flower of womanhood. She represents springtime and the uncertainty of youth, which is full of possibility and promise. Still unaware of herself and her strength, the Maiden is entrenched in family programming. Not yet committed to work, and dependent on relationships, she is vulnerable. Her most painful lessons come from her attachments--wanting to please and looking outside to others.

Persephone was the archetypal Maiden. Let's explore her myth.

Persephone was the beloved daughter of Demeter, Mother Goddess of Agriculture. She would play in the fields and gather flowers with her companions while her mother worked. One day, Persephone noticed a hundred-bloom narcissus flower of striking beauty. As she bent to pick up the flower, Gaia opened the Earth and, from the underworld, the God of Death rose up and abducted her. When Demeter heard her daughter's bitter cry for help, her heart was seized with sorrow.

Hades had stripped Persephone of her virginal innocence and drew her into the darkness, and she was powerless to avoid his violent penetration. Persephone was sorely vexed to find herself in the underworld and refused to eat.

As the ruler of the underworld and judge of the spirits of the dead, Hades' law was irrevocable. He was lonely and asked Zeus for the sweet Maiden to be his flowering bride, but he got her with the help of Gaia, the Earth Mother. The Romans called Hades, "Pluto," which means riches. His possessions included all the rich underground resources--the minerals, elements and gems of the world. None of that meant anything to the Maiden, who wanted only flowers, sunlight, friends and her mother.

For nine days and nights, Demeter searched far and wide for her daughter. Her feelings went from sadness to grief, then to depression, and finally to anger and rage. In desperation she asked Helios, the Sun who sees everything, where her daughter was. The news that her brother, Hades, had violated her child was infuriating. Deprived of her daughter and full of rage, Demeter neglected her duties as Mother Provider. Plants died and there was a great famine, but Demeter made it clear that she would not stop this blight until her daughter was safely returned.

Zeus finally intervened, sending Hermes to bring Persephone to her mother. The first question Demeter asked, after she was joyfully reunited with her daughter, was, "Did you eat anything while you were in the underworld?" She answered, "Yes, I had some pomegranate seeds." With freedom as bait, Pluto had lulled her into eating the seeds and, because she partook of the underworld, she was bound to it.

A compromise was then reached: Persephone would live for six months of the year with her mother, thus creating spring and summer, and for six months with her husband, creating fall and winter. The bargain was struck, and Persephone went willingly into the underworld to co-rule with her king.

The Maiden's story points to a love born out of pain. Becoming an individual entails separating from mother and squarely confronting feelings of isolation.

Hades forced the Maiden into darkness. As the ruler of the underworld, he represents those deeply buried layers of our psyche that are our unconscious workings. Any descent into the unconscious is a loss of innocence, but that is the first step of creation. Gaia, the Great

Mother, opened the Earth, permitting the Maiden access to the womb of the unconscious. It was a cruel yet necessary abduction for the development of her potential.

Invisible in the outer world, Pluto symbolizes our hidden parts--our compulsions and obsessions that speak loudly through shades of fascination and absorption. His entrance into consciousness always feels like a violation. Driven by strong desires, Hades pulls us out of life for either renewal or death. The forms may be apathy, discouragement, depression, loss of energy, or sickness. Our deeply buried emotions make relationships the battlefield until victory comes with conquering the self.

The voluntary eating of six pomegranate seeds marks the awakening of sexuality. Because the pomegranate contains mostly seeds, Western occult lore uses it to represent fertility. Hades entrapped Persephone into eating the seeds and becoming his wife, which shows the need to confront power and manipulation head on.

This story implies the need for periodic separation in relationships where there is a high degree of passion and intensity. Otherwise, we may merge with another, lose our identity, and neglect our own duties.

Despite the adversity, Persephone's marriage to the God of Death was a transformative experience that expanded her consciousness so that a broader spiritual love was possible.

This theme has profoundly affected my inner reality. I know Persephone, the innocent springtime maiden, intimately. I too picked the narcissus flower and suffered greatly from unconscious emotional abductions. My fulfillment came only after confronting deeply repressed emotions within my relationships and personally gaining self-esteem.

Acquiring Self-Esteem

Before Persephone was abducted she was a carefree girl, playing with her friends. When snatched from her mother she was gathering a narcissus bloom, the symbol of self-love. Self-love allows us to separate from the umbilical ties that bind us to mother, a necessary step in our preparation for adult mating. Self-love is the most basic ingredient for a healthy personality. There is no greater gift that we can give ourselves and, much as we wish it were so, no one else can give it to us.

We all experience love to some degree by feeling needed, but remember, no one needs you more than you need yourself. Value yourself by accepting yourself as you are now. Value your uniqueness. Release judgments. Stop whipping yourself with criticism and remorse. When doubts creep in, do not identify with the feelings they bring.

Self-love requires that you be true to yourself and share your truth with others. If you feel unloved, open your heart to love and appreciation. Give love to someone else and be open to receive it. Give to yourself everything you want from others. When you appreciate yourself, you are open to the truth--that the underlying Divine Spirit is in all of us.

Your true sense of self hides and is often different from your conscious image of yourself. The conscious view may be positive, but deep inside may lurk feelings of unworthiness. This lack of objectivity gives an inaccurate sense of self. For years I had a feeling of not being worthy. I had difficulty receiving. I knew intellectually that this was ridiculous, and I didn't want those feelings, but until I awakened my own love nature, I felt unloved. Enormously successful people have thought themselves "secretly unqualified." Richard Burton once described himself as "a Welsh farm boy, undeserving of his fame."

We have to get beyond our programs and even other people's reactions who may also harbor false perceptions. What you think about yourself is more important than what others think of you. Cast off the notion that people's opinions can affect your intrinsic self-worth. They can't!

Let the Goddess be your champion for building a positive self-image. Find your primary energy of love--nurturing, caring, unconditional love. Unconditional love requires constant appreciation, total forgiveness, and endless patience. Everyone needs love. Love is the universal solvent. All love starts with self-love. That is the grand paradox. It is only by loving yourself that you will receive the love and acceptance you want from others.

I have had to learn the principles of self-esteem, since my sense of self was not always good. Once, when it hit

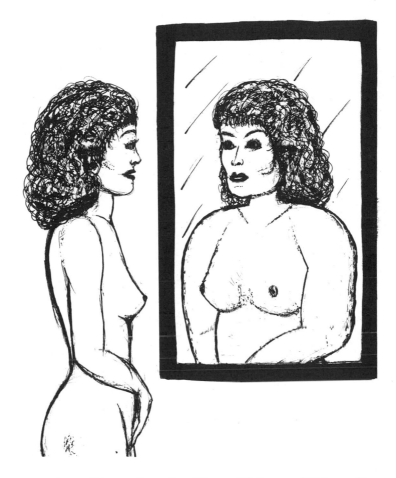

What You See Is Not Always What Is

bottom, the universe presented a perfect opportunity for my spiritual growth. I was scheduled to speak at the annual San Francisco Tarot Symposium. My topic was the Star card, which is the embodiment of self-esteem. I thought, "Thank you, Divine Mother. Again you have given me an opportunity to teach what I need most to learn." In preparation for my lecture, I turned inward and instructed my Maiden to use the principles of self-esteem and, like building blocks, to construct me a new "house." Over the years this house has been remodeled into a temple, and my Maiden has became the Goddess who dwells within.

Here is a list of ways to improve your self-image:

o   Start by conditioning your unconscious mind for success. Set "do-able deeds." Create little wins daily. The unconscious does not distinguish between details. Everything blends--a win is a win, no matter whether it is big or small. Make the smallest events important. Program your mind with victory and you will become a winner.

o   Do things that foster your creativity. Make a list of all the people, things, and events that support and feed your inner self.

o   Promise to do something every day that nourishes you. Let simple acts, like dressing, become a ritual of self-love. Give yourself treats and enough free time for play.

o   Trust yourself to listen to yourself, speak your truth, and follow your heart's desire.

o   Let go of all judgments. Walk with your shoulders back and your heart out. It is gesture that instills confidence.

o   Build your confidence by stretching and challenging yourself. Do something you are not sure you can do. If you fail the first time, don't give up. Set yourself the task again and again until you have mastered it.

o   Picture yourself in a positive light, emotionally secure, living in joy, and connected to your Source. Visualize the "real you" in as much detail as possible, and recall that image to your mind's eye throughout the day. Images are more powerful than words. They break through the barriers of the mind, penetrating into realms that lie beyond thought.

o   Love yourself each moment by asking yourself, "Does this situation win my approval?" or "Is this any way to love myself?" Self-love is not a wave upon which you can just sit back and ride. It must be renewed and recreated in every moment.

Becoming Your Own Caretaker

Acknowledge and respect your "emotional necessities" and take charge to see that they are fulfilled. No one will ever satisfy all our emotional needs, for everyone has their own unique evolutionary agenda. Remember, relationships do to us only what we do to ourselves. Blaming others, or circumstances in general, for our predicaments will never be emotionally healing.

You can find your heroic strength only by breaking dependencies and becoming your own Caretaker. Artemis, the Virgin who always remained true to herself, is again our model. You become your independent female spirit, when you follow your own inclinations and set your own goals.

We must also stop being a Caretaker for others. Ask yourself: *Where do I carry a load that is rightfully someone else's?* My client, Doris, agonizes over family issues. She always feels obligated to do things for her needy family. They openly depend on her for practical and economic support, and she accepts complete responsibility for them. She doesn't believe she even has a choice. Lately she has had financial problems, but even this has not stopped her from giving beyond her means. What she has set up for herself is "pain if you do and pain if you don't."

Doris resents her family's dependency but would feel guilty if she did not take care of them. Bound by the illusions of her mind, she feels compelled to give such things as wardrobes to her little niece, Christmas trips to her father, and health insurance to her sister. Because she is trapped by her feelings of obligation, she often protects herself by shutting down emotionally.

I tell Doris to close her purse and give from her heart. Doris' giving is out of balance. Everyone needs to act consciously from the inside out, not the other way around. Only then can we reverse automatic emotional reactions. Remember, it is not your responsibility to provide for another's pleasure nor to take away the pain, especially when giving someone else joy is won only by sacrificing your own. It is your responsibility to see that you get what you need.

If you wish to live in joy, you can. *Examine what gives you emotional security and comfort.* All emotional needs ultimately come from a deep desire for reunion with the God-force. Don't judge them. Opening to your emotional needs is necessary for fulfillment, but mastery comes only through practice, patience, and loving acceptance.

Wanting to Be Liked

The Maiden's desire is to please. Women in general are more inclined to accommodate and naturally go toward compromise and smoothing the rough spots in relationships. "I want what you want" is a sure way to get along with others, but that attitude as a constant companion makes us a pawn being cast about by the will of others. Being charming and full of sweetness and light may win "Miss Congeniality," but this, too, is part of the shadow. "Please like me" and "Is everybody happy?" are "power-sappers" that block intimacy and undermine our self-esteem.

You break this pattern by vowing to love yourself unconditionally, just because love is what you are. You do not have to earn it, it is the source of your being. Christ said: "Love thy neighbor as thy self." Love yourself, first and foremost.

Many people learned conditional love while growing up. It is a belief that says, "To successfully find love, I must fit an 'approved standard' and do 'acceptable' things." This belief programmed me to think my sole worth and goodness lay in my ability to fulfill the needs and wishes of others. The fear is that if we fail to please others, love will be withheld. When we live for others and not ourselves, our self-esteem erodes away, causing us to doubt our abilities.

Many women fall into a pattern of being lulled into habitual indifference, only to find their lives suddenly out of their hands. Does this sound familiar? He says, "What do you want to do?" She says, "I don't know, what do you want to do?" It's as if you do not have an opinion until you are sure it will be approved by others. I used to be like that in the beginning of a new relationship, but after getting better acquainted, I'd revert to the real, more assertive, me. After starting out with a kitten, few men were ready when the tiger leaped out. It took me many years to admit to myself that this survival mechanism was a manipulative act, even though it was unconscious and felt quite natural.

When I asked a client, who was a successful business-woman, the secret of her power, she said, "I always tried to please others. Now people try to please me. Instead of only considering what others wanted, I now figure out what I desire for myself. It's a difference in focus."

The soulmaking journey is always toward balance. Always being nice for the sake of peace sabotages our purpose and robs us of the opportunity to live to our fullest potential. When we listen to our feelings and follow with words or action, balance is achieved. If we ignore or subordinate any part of our nature, even to please others, we create a dangerous "back-pressure" of repressed action that will erupt unexpectedly and create damaging emotions.

Let this example show you what I mean: Many years ago a friend and his buddy came over to my house on their way to go camping. Because of my ever-pleasing nature, I served them generously. Soon it started to rain, and they decided to change their plans. My feelings were saying, "Well, that's enough company for me!" Yet, I remember my mind debating with those feelings: "Be nice, it wouldn't be gracious to say, 'Go home!'" They stayed and stayed and as time passed I began to feel used. In my mind, I started picking on them. I wasn't aware that they were doing to me only what I was doing to myself. I ignored my true feelings, so they ignored them as well. People only do to you what you do to yourself. I timidly let the situation go on until I got angry. By then my feelings were so strong that with fury I spoke out. This whole uncomfortable situation could have easily been avoided. If I had stopped giving on an energy level, they might have gotten the hint, and if not, then I could have said courteously, "Well, it's been a fun visit, but now I need some space."

Listen to your feelings and know there is a way to speak the truth and be kind at the same time. A Goddess Warrior's golden rule is: Express your heartfelt feelings, let them go, let them flow. Stop caring for others by sacrificing yourself. People value you only to the degree you value yourself. Value yourself and your time. Do not let other people waste your time either. If you're like most of us, you don't need anyone's help with that.

Moving Beyond the Maiden of Desire

There is one thing we all seek and that is happiness, although it may come in different forms of desire. Desire is a natural yearning. Hindu mythology tells us that the first thing that arose was desire. Desire precedes creation. Desire is an intense magnet, for our destiny is the result of all the choices we make, and our choices are always based upon our desires being filled.

The following process will show how to clear the mental blocks that inhibit you from achieving your desires: *Determine what you want, in as much detail as possible.* Trust your ability to draw your desires into your space, and then be open to receive them. Remember, go for the essence, not for the form. Release who, when, where, and how you want your desires.

Aphrodite is the Maiden of Desire, but her dark side is the **Temptress**. If you do not avoid temptation, you will be seduced into wrong associations, materialism, and overindulgences. Learn balance from this Queen of Balance or your desire for well-being turns to greed, and your love of beauty fades into vanity.

The two sides of a Temptress are: "Iwanna" and "Gimme." Hers is the key to that form of happiness obtained through satisfaction of material desire. But sadly, this satisfaction is not without its price. Satisfying some of your desires is all too often like making a monkey trap. If you haven't trapped a monkey lately here's how:

Find a hollow gourd about the size of a cantaloupe and cut a hole the size of a half dollar in one side and two holes the size of a dime in the other. Pass a cord through the two small holes and tie it to a tree. Then, put a spoonful of uncooked rice or grain inside the gourd. When a monkey finds the gourd and smells the grain, it will squeeze its hand inside the hole by elongating its fingers. When it scoops up the grain and tightly closes its fist, its hand will not fit back through the opening. The monkey is stuck fast and will not let go. An open, empty hand could easily slip back out,

The Maiden and Her Many Possibilities

but not with a fist full of grain. Because the monkey will not let go of the object of its desire, it allows itself to be captured and eaten.

Do not let the desires of your beast be your motivating force. Otherwise you will be controlled through your appetites. Some desires lead us to self-improvement, some lead to pain. The problem comes when the preponderance of our desires is dedicated to the behests of our beast.

Many people believe their survival and their fulfillment
come in the satisfaction of acquiring material possessions.
As we evolve, we refine our desires. We learn that the
chain we use to bind our desires to us is the chain that
binds us to them. It doesn't matter whether those chains
are of iron or gold--they bind just as tightly.

Ken Keyes said in his *Handbook to Higher Consciousness* that the secret to lasting happiness is to
change all desires from needs to preferences. When an
overwhelming desire pops up, say to yourself, "That might
be great, but only if it be Thy will." Then let go of all
attachment to the outcome. When you take away the
obsessions created by your expectations, you free yourself
from being controlled and disappointed.

Swami Satchidananda tells us that chasing after
desire is like chasing our own shadow. No matter how
fast we run, it's always a step ahead. When we grow tired
of chasing after it, stop and turn to go, we see the light of
the Sun. It was there all the time. Now, no matter how
fast we run toward the light, our shadow will run after us
crying, "Hey! Remember me? Don't leave me behind."

Stop chasing those desires that promise happiness
and always elude you. When you renounce the fruitless
search for fleeting desire and turn toward the true source
of energy, the Light of your soul, the world starts running
after you with money, position, relationships, fame, or
whatever your desires might be.

15

Allowing Mothers's Choice

In every culture around the world, motherhood is a sacred rite. Being a mother in itself fulfills the Hero's Journey. As a discipline toward higher consciousness, motherhood demands constant selfless service. Nothing teaches unconditional love like motherhood.

It is important to teach children by constantly setting a positive example. Small children take life literally. There is great joy in helping a helpless infant grow into a mature man or woman. Mothers have the greatest influence in this miraculous transformation. Becoming a mother takes sacrifice and life-long commitment. It should not be taken lightly.

Demeter, the Mother Goddess of Grain

The essence of maternal instinct comes from what the Greeks worshiped in Demeter. She was a generous, bountiful **Mother Goddess of Grain and Agriculture**. Known as **Ceres** to the Romans, she was linked with Persephone to fit the traditional roles of mother and daughter. Bolen describes these Vulnerable goddesses as having a quality of consciousness that is like "diffused radiant light." This light, like a generalized attention, allows for feeling the nuances in others. It is how a mother hears the whimpering of her child through a lot of space and conversation. Demeter represents the unconditional love of a mother for her child. Both her child rearing and her gardening roles entail care and cultivation over a period of time. Yet, just as with modern mothers, where the economy demands that they work outside the home, it was necessary for Demeter to neglect her child while she carried out her life's work.

Demeter is the essence of the maternal instinct, which gets fulfilled through pregnancy. Yet there are other ways to satisfy this archetype within, such as cooking food, gardening, teaching the young, working in the healing professions, and of course mothering your own Inner Child.

The Right to Motherhood

Before the general distribution of birth control, women were expected to quietly fulfill the role of mother when it was thrust upon them. The old myth says that all women have maternal instincts and automatically know how to be loving mothers, they instinctively know how to do the best for each child. Being a mother was considered the essence of being a woman. If we did not choose motherhood as a life work or failed to conceive, we failed as women. This reproductive programming, imprinted in every woman, becomes an unconscious craving in our twenties and an anxiety in our thirties. Yet this powerful program has now become detrimental to the health of our planet. We have to realize that there is a population problem and we no longer need to keep having babies for our survival.

It is not only our right but our duty to choose. Today, in the age of choice, we can defeat this programming. If you are feeling the urge for motherhood, ask for deep insight. Is this urge just a species survival program, or is it your true path of Learning? Choose consciously.

The truth is that becoming a mother is a process that takes a considerable period of adjustment. A client said, "It's an art you learn like any other skill." Having a child is an intense emotional and physical experience. It assures that a woman will never be the same again. In pregnancy there is a complete hormonal changeover that prepares a woman for the task ahead. Often she loses control of her body and has feelings of depression and vulnerability. Pregnancy is especially stressful in these modern times, for woman lack the community support systems they had in the past. To give her infant a sense of security, a woman must give up her independence and change her identity. Many women delay motherhood to work on their careers. Others choose not to sacrifice their careers at all. Those who choose motherhood often feel a mixture of love and anger toward their children.

One of my clients expressed turmoil and resentment from the constant interruptions and demands of her small child. She felt out of control and yet terribly guilty for having these feelings. She said, "Being a mother is a paradox. My child gives me the opportunity to give selflessly, but he also keeps me form doing things I need to do for myself. It's a double edged sword, for he brings out my best and my worst." Even though she wanted a child, when he came she was not prepared for her feelings. Nevertheless, he is her pride and joy.

A childless client who was approaching middle age came to me for counseling. "Should I have a child before it's too late?" she asked. One part of her craved the love and companionship of a baby, but the other side feared the restrictions and responsibilities it would bring. To help her solve her problem, she went "inside" herself and imagined taking two separate journey, one for each choice. As she visualized the childless path, she felt as if she were cruising on a freeway, but she was lonely. Something was missing. The other path was an old country road. It wasn't as fast and efficient, but it was comfortable, richer, and more colorful. She emerged from her meditation with her turmoil gone. Her feelings and a simple mental image revealed her deep desire to be a mother.

Another client recently pondered about having a baby. She was in her early thirties with two daughters, ages seven and eight. She was aspiring to be a singer and was happily studying with the best teacher in the area. But she said, "When I work toward singing, I'm striving, but when I am breast feeding I am being there." In spite of this, she came to understand that two children were enough and that it was time to focus on her career.

When I was growing up, motherhood appeared like a lot of drudgery: Mom's role seemed to be servant and policeman. My mother went to work in the family business when I was two years old. As the youngest child, my programming allowed me to identify more strongly with Persephone, whereas my two sisters and my mother followed the Demeter role. Unconsciously I knew I did not want the role of mother. This was evident in my senior year of college, when part of a home-management course was to care for an infant. I broke out with a cold sore and was relieved of the job. But if circumstances were different I, like many others, may have "slipped" into the mother role without conscious thought. For me motherhood was not my path, although my strong maternal instincts get played out by providing psychological and spiritual nourishment to my clients. My "babies" are my creative projects.

I have worked with several women who had strong maternal instincts and allowed it to result in multiple unwanted pregnancies. Because they deeply wanted the love of a child, they unconsciously kept creating pregnancies. Having an abortion is a loaded moral issue. Yet if an unwanted pregnancy occurs, know that you have that option. I feel an abortion might be seen as a spiritual "misdemeanor," not a "felony."

The Right to Abort

Any woman unwillingly thrust into the role of motherhood can develop a deep sense of resentment that is often damaging to both mother and child. Time magazine reported in 1987, "Over a million American teenagers become pregnant every year and four out of five are not married."

Of all the influences that can destroy the golden potential of a life, let alone what it does to the child, an ill-timed pregnancy is one of the greatest. Birth control, other than tubal ligation or vasectomy, is never 100 percent reliable. Some forms of birth control, such as birth control pills, can even be harmful. They affect both weight and the ability to digest sugar and starch, giving a greater chance of developing diabetes.

I was reminded of the cliche, "We've come a long way, baby!" when my 69-year-old neighbor told me a sad tale of her "old days." When my neighbor was in her thirties, her friend Maria got pregnant. Maria's two daughters were already nine and ten. The thought of starting all over again, when her children were just old enough to allow her a personal life, was terrifying. She decided she wanted an abortion, but her husband forbade it. Not only was her husband against abortion, but her doctor, relatives and friends told her, "You can't kill that poor helpless child." Forced to have a child she did not want turned this story into one of life's tragedies. The child seemed to agree with her on some level, because he lived for only three years. Maria's husband not only controlled her action but began cheating on her. Overwhelmed by everything, she ended up committing suicide.

This is a dire drama that dives home the importance of women having sovereignty over themselves and following their inner feelings. We have to trust ourselves and know we have a choice, unlike our sisters of the past. Yet I shiver as I hear our politicians taking our rights away. We need to fight this survival programming that lurks deep within our beast. We must stop it from becoming reinforced with strict moral conditioning and fortified with male authority and legal precedent.

An abortion is not a frivolous experience. A therapeutic abortion is expensive and emotionally taxing. The body goes through a complete hormonal change, which often feels like an emotional sleigh ride. For women with strong maternal instincts and rigid moral beliefs, the experience can be emotionally painful and sometimes damaging.

A client timidly asked me if I thought the universe punished us for our wrongdoings. For years she felt she has suffered for the "sin" of having an abortion. A bodyworker friend said, "Several women I have worked on seem to have suffered from a soul sickness that could be traced back to their abortions." Violating our moral taboos can create deep emotional scars. After an abortion, competent counseling may be necessary to heal feelings of remorse, guilt and regret.

All challenges are opportunities to grow, and choosing to have an abortion is not different. If it happens to you, look deep within to find the roots of those creative impulses that led to the creation of a new life. Here is a case in point:

Caroline's Story

I once counseled a client who had magically and inadvertently created an unwanted pregnancy. Caroline had felt that she wanted to expand her creativity and to be more effectual in the world. To help focus her mind and improve her creative energy, she began reciting the affirmation, "I want new life in me--My creativity is being born." Caroline made a drawing of the Empress, a maternal archetype from the tarot, and hung it in her room, ironically, for nine months. Picturing the birth of her creativity did create new life. She conceived a child.

Having this child would have been a major tragedy in her life. Not only was she single, but she had not had sex in more than a year when she succumbed to the enticement of a former lover. They made love only once, but that was quite enough to remind her how completely unsuitable he was for her. Moreover, she was just getting started in her career and was barely able to support herself. Caroline made some fundamental errors that got her "into trouble." Besides having a casual liaison with the "wrong man," she dabbled with a form of magic she knew nothing about. Her affirmations became an incantation for the unwanted pregnancy.

Our story has a happy ending, however, as Caroline found in this experience an opportunity to release old emotional attachments. Soon after her abortion, Caroline had a new beginning, which was full of positive growth.

The universe teaches us that every adversity has an equal or greater benefit.

A Goddess Warrior becomes accountable for her desires, thoughts, and beliefs. Choice means becoming responsible for ourselves and what happens to us. It means taking charge and being willing to have it a new way, no matter what the situation looks like. Every woman needs to make her own personal choices. No one should choose for us. Let's make sure we keep it that way.

16

The Womanly Wonders of Venus

Real power comes when we identify with Venus, the Goddess in possession of womanly wonders. Venus--**Aphrodite**, to the Greeks--is the essence of love, fertility, and creativity. She represents the source of reproductive energy of the universe. Her astonishing bounty exists within everyone, for she represents our inner creative abundance. A rich, fertile garden full of vegetables, fruits, and flowers is her image.

Her face shines as **Shakti, Creative Lover, Beautiful Courtesan, Vision Carrier, Tantrika, Scarlet Woman**, and the **Bringer of Joy**. She creates her world through the vehicle of love--the underlying support of the physical universe. To become the Goddess of Love, dedicate yourself to expressing love, beauty, and joy in all you do. Become the essence of Love.

Venus loves by getting into the moment with no thought of an outcome. She chooses love for itself and not for what it brings. As an **Alchemical Goddess**, she favors change and process to permanence. From her we learn to live in the present and sharpen our awareness on whatever we are doing in the moment, giving no concern to the goal.

Venus "consciousness" is a focused awareness that is simultaneously passive and active. Jean Bolen compares her to limelight in a theater, which helps enhance, dramatize, and magnetize emotional involvement with the characters on the stage. As we identify with Venus, we make others feel fascinating and important. The womanly wonders exist in people who like people. The effects are not just romantic sexual love, but also deep friendship, soul connection, and true empathetic understanding and rapport.

Venus operates through the emotional body. She lures us into the unconscious to a new intuitive understanding that lies beyond the realm of rational thought. Socrates believed Aphrodite to be a form of "divine madness," far superior to normal sanity. Her desire is to blissfully "know and be known." Her special favor is infusing life with warmth, affection, and creativity, which bind together in harmony and in pleasure. She is the magnetic force of attraction. I experience the wonders of Venus as a great blessing in my personality and in my relationships.

Invoking Female Magnetism

Aphrodite is the epitome of all that is female. She exudes charm and gracious receptivity and draws to herself what she wants. In return, she gives pleasure, enjoyment, and beauty. According to the Greeks, Aphrodite was the most beautiful of all goddesses, graced from birth with a perfect figure, a gorgeous face, and a pleasant smile. Her alluring magnetism created a magically seductive aura. Only the strongest could resist her powerful, sweet spell.

Aphrodite was created spontaneously when Cronus (Saturn) castrated his father, Ouranos (Uranus), and cast his genitals into the sea. From them she was born in the deep ocean, fully grown, and floated to the surface dressed only in white foam. Aphrodite started life already the epitome of ripe sexuality. She needed no man to initiate her into womanhood. She gave of herself freely but could never be raped or forced against her will. Aphrodite's pure essence was attraction and passionate love.

As you identify with this Goddess, you awaken the great power of female magnetism. Imagine that each cell of your body is a source of magnetic attraction and that your heart is the most powerful magnet of all.

Turn On Your Powers of Attraction and Feel Your Magnetic Womanly Wonders

By invoking the Goddess you become irresistible. Know that you already have within you the ability to draw to you your heart's desire. Never underestimate this power of creative attraction, for it is the force of life itself.

Opening the Heart to Receive

A Goddess Warrior infuses love into life in responsible ways. To find more love in the universe, no matter where you are, you must open yourself to love, even if it is challenging. When you open your heart, you enhance your capacity to draw deep and intimate love from others as well as to increase your love of God. The choice is yours. When you awaken self-trust you will find that connecting with others becomes easier every day.

Love grows from a day-to-day openness and sharing. Yet, often we unconsciously hide our love and create a life of emptiness. Many people are conditioned to believe that no one will love them, and because of their belief, they receive no love. They tend to exaggerate the importance of mating and diminish the importance of friendship. Thoughts of unworthiness or hostility also block the Goddess channels and deepen our sense of isolation.

Whenever you decide you want more love in your life, you can easily get it by connecting with people through your heart. Do it as a conscious gesture and see the amazing results. Try extending your heart to strangers, at the gas station and at the grocery store. Try it with salesclerks as well as with your friends, and watch love flow into your life. People will automatically feel a warmth and caring for you, even if they do not know why.

If you are an instrument of love in this world, all barriers will dissolve before you. The illusion of separateness will vanish, revealing a network of beings whose nature is infinite joy. It's only a matter of time.

Once a policeman stopped me. When I asked him what I did wrong, he said, "Where should I start? You went the wrong way down a one way street; you were going 35 mph in a 25 mph zone...." I looked him in the eyes and said, "Please don't give me a ticket," and telepathically poured love into his heart. After explaining at considerable length the extent of my traffic sins, he said, "I really don't know why I am not giving you a ticket."

Another time I connected in the heart with an auto repairman who gave me emergency road service. He went beyond the call of duty to help me. He even waited to follow my car to make certain I would be all right. He gave me so much nurturing care that I could have been his daughter. As you break the barriers of separateness between yourself and others, you open your heart to receive and you open the hearts of others to give.

Open Your Heart

Being Willing to Receive

The key to having more love and pleasure is a willingness to receive as well as to give. If you want to receive more, give to yourself. Make it happen! Energy follows thought, so put your attention on receiving.

When I was teaching self-esteem, each week I focused consciously on one thought. One affirmation was, "I am opening to receive love from anywhere in the universe." That week I received two appreciative letters from clients telling me of the effectiveness of my work, three calls from men out of my past, kind words from friends and strangers, and special attention from the kitty, who constantly insisted on being on my lap. The next week I became even more aware of receiving when I focused on, "I am open to receive any good thing the universe has for me." That week I received a diamond ring from a friend. Another friend brought me a huge, gorgeous, antique marble Quan Yin, the Goddess of Mercy. I then found presents, baskets, and trinkets at my door. I was amazed at the power of my intention and grateful for what I had been given.

My clients have learned to use this process. One example, which produced immediate feedback, came from a woman driving home from a session. While she was thinking about opening to receive love, a man in a passing car started communicating with her through hand held signs that expressed, "Hi! You are beautiful. Are you free?" She said that when she directed her intent, her lover always became more attentive. You will be amazed at the power of directing your will toward receiving.

Acknowledging Appreciation

To awaken your womanly wonders, start your day by appreciating the little things: the hot water in the bath, the taste of toothpaste, the smell of coffee, and so on. You cannot hold onto satisfaction; it must be recreated from moment to moment. Therefore, take time to appreciate yourself and others. *Write down some of life's pleasantries and the joys you share in common with others.* Recognize those special people in your life with words of praise. Say "I love you" often. Compliment them daily. Make them feel important, and they will act magnanimously toward you. All people or things have value only in proportion to how much you appreciate them. Besides, the only way to live happily with people is to overlook their faults and admire their virtues.

Identifying with the Goddess brings increase, for possessing an "attitude of gratitude" always makes space for more. When you treat everyone with love and respect, you always remain in harmony with your human relationships--neither ruling nor being ruled.

Honoring the Temple

We awaken our womanly wonders by first making the Goddess connection within ourselves. In complete agreement with Christ and Buddha, Venus considers the body to be a holy creation--the sacred temple of the soul. She is unashamed and uninhibited and by nature possesses raw sensuality.

Venus teaches us to accept our bodies and helps us to let go of the desire for unattainable perfection. Often we have the habit of focusing on those parts of our bodies that are less than perfect.

Too many people have bought into the social standard that only a thin athletic body is attractive. Beauty is relative. It is an energy, an aliveness that only comes by living from inside out.

Appreciate the beauty of your body, by learning not to judge it. Give attention to what you like about yourself. Your body will respond to this appreciation by growing increasingly more attractive. If this is difficult, start by finding beauty in others who have a similar body type. It is how you carry yourself, rather than your size or shape, that makes you beautiful.

Being Beautifully Creative

The creative process belongs to the Goddess, for it is much like being in love. Creativity is a sensual process where our attention is intensely focused on the here and now. It is an enlivening experience, an invigorating exchange that gives birth to something new. Venus represents the spark of Divine Creation that infuses thought with inspiration to create the Golden Child. Her power of imagination is the foundation of all creation and the key to physical manifestation. Artistic creativity parallels the creation of life, for both processes include attraction, union, fertilization, incubation, and birth.

The Goddess teaches us to follow our bliss--to find the inner source of true creativity--that fertilizes a joyous delivery. Find a creative project where you can focus your love nature into a daily dedication to the Goddess.

During my early years as a flight attendant, I taught myself to create macrame. I would fill long hours of waiting developing my craft. At first I learned to make plant holders and necklaces and then went on to create huge tapestries. Something else is born during the creative process. New channels are opened for problem solving and self-acceptance. Macrame unlocked my creative potential, whereas Walter opened his with music. Any creative expression will do.

When you unlock your creativity in one area, you can use the knowledge gained to bring creativity into any other endeavor. I never believed I could draw until I bought some oil pastels and started. Whenever we use our hands creatively, our inner nature begins pouring out. Perhaps not at first, but with love and patience anyone can open the doors to untapped creative re-sources. For a while my home looked like a small child was living there. My creative attempts were pinned to doors, walls, and cupboards. To my amazement, I became fairly good. I wouldn't say the great galleries of the world were clamoring to bid for my masterpieces, but the process was a profound healing for my Inner Child. Let your latent artist come out; it will awaken the Goddess.

Venus' special gift is to evoke the beauty that she sees within. Become her and glory in your unique attractiveness. Appreciate your natural self, yet take those extra few minutes to enhance your appearance. The act of adornment is a way of refining yourself and making the most of what you were given.

An esthetically pleasing decor with objects of art, paintings, and flowers is an expression of the Goddess. Let your own personal expression of artistic creativity be a dedication to the Goddess.

Find and acknowledge your Goddess within. Align your womanly wonders to Venus' highest vibrations, and let her powers flow through you. Let this Alchemical Goddess fill you with the desire to do good for all humanity. When you become a Goddess with the intent of being a vehicle of her Divine nature, life becomes productive, fruitful, and abundant.

Memorize the following verse as an invocation:

I am Venus--Lover, Mother, Tart and Tease

As the creator of pleasure, my aim is to please.

Joy is my season, appreciation, my day.

Balance is my measure, and love, the way.

17

One need not go to the mountain top to commune with Divinity. Its temple is the body. Its sacrament the communion between lovers.

John Mumford

The Powers of a Sexual Woman

Woman is the custodian of the creative force and the embodiment of sensuality. The keys to eroticism are hidden within her nature. It is our eroticism that allows change and will create a new renaissance. Womanly wonders is another name for the erotic bounty of the female. Once it awakens, woman's sexuality is limitless and multidimensional.

In the personality, female sexuality is called Venus. She is Shakti, a wondrous power that leads to the ecstasy of fulfillment when aroused. This life-infusing energy of woman ignites the fires of creative potential. Attainment of desire, knowledge, and blissful enjoyment of the erotic arts are all blessings that she grants.

Let Touching Replace Consuming

We satisfy our need for sensual gratification by touching and being touched. If we do not get enough touching, we may covertly fulfill this desire by too much eating, drinking, or shopping. Every time a certain friend came to my house, she headed straight for the refrigerator. It was comical, because it was such persistent, unconscious

behavior. She stopped only when I began touching her
arm or hair, for what she really was coming to me for was
a loving connection. How often is going for those sweets a
cry for love? Chocolate is especially "sinful," because it
contains a neuropeptide that is similar to a natural che-
mical produced by the brain when we are in love.

Elevating Sexuality

The sexual aspect of ourselves needs to be elevated out
of darkness into light. We transform any guilty puritanical
repression, when we learn to experience our sexuality as a
natural wilderness adventure. Mathew Fox in a *Common
Boundary* interview said, "When we celebrate lovemaking
as playing in the Garden of Eden, we bring a feeling of
mystism and sacredness to ourselves. The Eskimo's word
for lovemaking is 'to make laughter together.' You have
this (attitude) in *Song of Songs* (a Sufi book of wisdom),
which ends with a woman saying to her lover, 'Come, play
on the mountains.' Mountain in Hebrew means 'breast';
she had a sense of her body as cosmic. It's an incredible
sensual experience; its a cosmological invitation."

The sex drive is more then physical; it is the same
force as our spiritual energy. Properly disciplined, its force
propels us onward toward the Grand Consummation of
spiritual unity. In fact, the sexual disciplines of Tantra are
some of the oldest known methods of achieving God realization. It is a grand paradox that open, sensual, transmuted sexual love can free the soul from carnal bondage.

Too often people cut off their natural sexual impulses,
fearing where that energy might take them. Because of
this, many people, even in committed relationships, will
be shy, modest, or sexually uninterested. Judeo-Christian
theology has for centuries taught a doctrine of bodily
shame. Theologians have excised God from the body and
from nature, creating a split between the mind and body.
They taught that the beginning of all sin was to be found
within the body of woman. If women were not categorized
as the Madonna, then they were the Whore.

Once, when I was writing affirmations about the Godli-
ness of the body, I unconsciously wrote "Godlessness." I
was shocked, but it showed me how deep our conditioning
runs. Even though we believe in the enjoyment of sexua-

lity and appreciate the beauty of the body, underneath it all there may still lurk the belief that sex is sinful. The repressive conditionings of the past can be deep.

Madeline, who was raised in a religious atmosphere, came to me with a painful internal conflict. Her husband told her that, if she wanted it, he would pay for plastic surgery to enlarge her undeveloped breasts. Madeline had always accepted her boyish build. It rather suited her to be sexually understated. When she realized she could have a perfectly proportioned body, her Venus subpersonality was delighted and jumped at the suggestion, but another deeply devout self, whom she called Mary, felt it was a shameful taboo. She feared people would think of her as vain and unspiritual: a fallen woman.

After considerable internal dialogue between Venus and Mary, Madeline learned the secret of overcoming fear: being afraid, but doing it anyway. Her operation became an initiation ceremony that reduced her need to fear by removing her worn-out beliefs. Venus won, and Madeline and her husband are happy with her proportionally beautiful new body.

Let the Goddess express herself through you and eliminate the guilt that inhibits your love nature and blocks your creative energy. We have the right as human beings to express sexual energy and fulfill the desires of our hearts.

Deena Metzger, in an *Utne* article entitled, "Re-vamping the World: On the return of the Holy Prostitute," says we need to become vamps, sexually spiritual beings that must act out of eros. In early mythology a Temple Virgin meant a Temple Harlot or Sacred Prostitute. Her role was that of a Priestess who cleansed and restored men to their divine connection. In ancient Greece a woman who practiced sexual worship was respectfully called a Hetaera Woman or a Divine Courtesan. These women were once considered "the doorway to God," but now are condemned as fallen women or whores. It is sad that the role of sexual Goddess is so poorly understood in society.

When you activate the Goddess, behold your powers of physical attraction and that special "chemistry" that forms relationships. Awakening your Goddess stimulates erotic connections and the deeper meaning of sexuality. The key is living passionately by trusting and following your heart. The more we operate from inner truth the more alive and spontaneous we will be.

Eroticly Connecting Within the Taboos

The biggest blocks to expressing sexuality revolve around taboos. Taboos are beliefs that control behavior to further the cause of evolution through reducing risk to the individual or species. Most taboos have outlived their usefulness, but some are very resilient. The taboo against promiscuity has proven to be universally true. Free love is scary when you realize that, within recorded history, there have been only about forty years when there has not been a killer venereal disease loose upon the planet. Today sex is a deadly proposition once again. We live under the curse of incurable AIDS. This retro-virus packs a double whammy: not only can we get the disease ourselves but, because we carry it so long before symptoms manifest, we can infect others. The only foolproof system for avoiding disease is to limit sexuality to within a closed loop.

If you are a single Goddess Warrior, awaken your erotic womanly wonders by opening your heart and your sensuality, and when the desire for sexuality comes, be sure to practice safe sex. It helps, too, to know the difference between love and lust, which is fundamental to understanding human sexuality.

Distinguishing Love From Lust

Sexual energy is all pervasive. Venus is the creative life force that awakens in adolescence, when our bodies are racing toward adulthood. At this time, we are most easily swept off our feet by the wrong signals and accelerated into a fit of sexual frenzy that drives us to satisfy our biological needs. Sexuality can be cut off from emotional closeness, leaving behind only the lust to satisfy physical appetites, which is experienced as orgasmic release. Without discipline, an undeveloped Venus lures us into falling in and out of love easily, being the living embodiment of "love 'em and leave 'em." The modern tragedy is that many people mistaken strong emotional and physical impulses for true and abiding love.

Lust and love are antitheses of each other. Love thrives on familiarity and comfort; lust thrives on newness. Lust is a fire that fuels our grosser passions. Love is from the heart--that spark of the Divine Flame that ennobles our lives, transmuting eros into the alchemical rose of divine love.

Love is not an emotion. Love is what we are. Love is sharing. But love should never be the only reason we mate. When we open our hearts to love, we love everyone. One problem with the word "love" is that it has too many diverse meanings. The Greeks had four separate words for it, and the Hindus have several more. In the sense of a deep, interpersonal relationship, love is a choice and commitment, and should be made only after considerable deliberation. Traditionally, men have opened their hearts through their lust, whereas women opened their lust through their hearts. The Goddess, in the form of the Scarlet Woman, bridges love and lust into a sexual communication of bliss.

Becoming a Scarlet Woman

The way we can overcome our obsolete sexual patterns is to bring the idea of sacredness to our passions and to our bodies. Merge the Madonna with the Whore and become the Scarlet Woman. Remove the laws and taboos that bar you and become not only a vehicle of pleasure but also a blissful conduit to the Goddess. The Scarlet Woman is a Western occult symbol. As a **Tantrika,** she practices with a partner the sexual Tantra. The yogis call it the path of *Kaulacharya* . Gifted in the erotic arts of love, she uses her limitless sexual energy to excite and amplify the male potential. Joyfully, she maintains their combined potencies in a state of continuous arousal. The Scarlet Woman identifies with her lust but never loses sight of her love and devotion to God. She achieves a state of dynamic balance, a poise that opens her to explore her vast creative potential. Unite your virgin with your vixen and transform yourself into a Scarlet Women.

I am the Scarlet Woman,

Called both Goddess and Whore.

Astride my steed of Crimson fire

I devour the void, I am the door.

Scarlet irredesence my inner glow,

Love, my one desire.
Peace and Joy to those who know,
Those who have tasted my fire.
In the Center of bliss,
I lie with Sun and Moon above
Bathed in their nectar filled rays,
My only thought is love.

Female Sexual Potential

Women are gifted with greater sexual capacity than men. The myth of Tiresias vividly portrays this fact:

Tiresias was walking through the forest one day when he saw two serpents copulating. As he placed his staff between them, he changed into a woman and lived as a female for many years. Some years later, Tiresias went into the forest. Again she saw two snakes copulating, placed her staff between them, and immediately transformed back into a man.

One day on Mount Olympus, Zeus and Hera were having an argument about who enjoyed sex more, a man or a woman. Zeus believed women enjoyed it more, which was the excuse he gave Hera for needing more than one woman. Zeus felt that he should be allowed to make up in volume what he naturally lacked in intensity. Hera wasn't buying it, so they asked all the god/ess for their opinions, but none had known more than one sex.

Finally someone said, "Let's ask Tiresias he'll have to know." Tiresias' answer came back in a flash. "Why, the woman, of course nine times more than any man."

This answer displeased Hera, who struck Tiresias blind for this observation, but Zeus felt responsible for Tiresias' plight and gave him the gift of prophecy to offset his blindness.

The story of Tiresias affirms woman's sexual potential, whereas Aphrodite describes woman's sexual powers. Woman's sexuality is multidimensional.

There is still much to learn about female sexual potential. During the '60s, there was considerable controversy over whether the female orgasm was clitoral, vaginal, or both. We now know that both types of orgasm are possible. Dr. Grafenberg, a gynecologist, wrote about an erotically sensitive spot within women, commonly known as the G-spot. This was a brilliant discovery for twentieth-century science, but for millennia the tantric tradi-tion has called it the "sacred spot."

It may be difficult to find your sacred spot without the help of a partner. Located on the outer anterior wall of the vagina, it is halfway between the pubic bone and cervix. It feels like a lump, which varies in size from that of a small bean to a half dollar. It swells when stimulated. It is most often reached during lovemaking when the woman is on top or mounted from behind. It can also be manually stimulated by hand or with specially shaped vibrators.

When the G-spot is first stimulated, a woman often feels a slight desire to urinate, due to its nearness to the bladder. But, within a few seconds, that sensation vanishes and it becomes very pleasurable.

The sacred spot is more than physical. It is also a psychological point of opening and receptivity. For some, stimulating it brings up past, repressed feelings of pain and guilt. If this happens to you, merge with the point of pain and open to the support of your partner. You will quickly move through the vulnerability to a place of bliss and unity.

Glorifying the Mound of Venus

Another method of finding the joy aspect of the Goddess is by glorifying the vagina. Personify it as the altar of love. Called, "Yoni," she is the perfumed garden, and the Mound of Venus. In Tantric tradition, the sex organs are depicted on amulets as charms for worship. Tantrikas believe the "Gateway to Life" resides within the body of woman. The vagina is the purest, most sacred part of a woman's body because it is the source of all life. We are all the fruit of the womb, and "every man strives to reenter it through sexual contact."

Sexual secretions are the nectar of love. In ancient times they were called the "Elixir of Life" and were believed to be infused with both magical and psycho-physical properties. Wilhelm Reich proved that female sexual secretions were a special electrolytic emulsion that aided the generation and flow of electromagnetic energy during intercourse.

Nature designed aroma into the female essence as a stimulant. This oily, musky, water based emulsion is different at various times of the month. Too many people have an attitude that it is dirty or disgusting. If there is any unpleasant odor, it is because of some abnormality such as poor hygiene or an infection. Eliminate any fear of unpleasantness, by making yourself as desirable as possible by bathing before lovemaking.

Oral sex is natural and wonderful. Many consider it the epitome of eroticism. When we worship at the Mound of Venus, with tenderness and devotion, she will bestow upon us great bliss and ecstasy. Since the woman is slower to arouse, oral lovemaking can be the great equalizer. Oral stimulation helps focus the mind. Lack of focus is the principal reason women have difficulty achieving orgasm. Women have to gain control of their minds to achieve orgasm, whereas men must control their minds to avoid it.

Tapping Our Internal Fires

As we evolve, it is necessary to control Venus and her desire to possess all things. If we direct our life force only into the sex drive, it dissipates in orgasm--sort of a spiritual short-circuit. Uncontrolled, Venus can stir our passions, distract us from our higher purpose, and make it impossible to focus the mind. We overcome by moving beyond her world of glamour and appearances and by unlocking the creative spirit within.

Tapping the Goddess connects us with the great urge for consummation. When we surrender to love and passion, we open our astral channels and allow our *kundalini,* or life force, to flow.

Aphrodite's marriage to Hephaistos (Vulcan), the divine but crippled blacksmith, explains this fact. They seem poorly matched, for she was forever unfaithful to him and found many men to console her, especially Ares (Mars) who became her life-long lover. Why a perfect beauty would marry an ill-formed mate is understandable, if you consider that her domain was creativity and Vulcan was the most gifted of all heavenly artisans. He also depicts part of her shadow and her work.

Vulcan was the God of Terrestrial Fire, that ancient plasma that allowed mankind to live in colder climates, cook food, work with metal, and advance the process of civilization. His limping represents the zig-zag pattern of lightning. He was the God of Thunder who forged the great thunderbolt. The thunderbolt symbolizes the kundalini energy--the pure life force or internal fires--that powers the body as it lies sleeping at the base of the spine.

It is dangerous to release kundalini too soon and un-guided. This powerful sexual force is often described as looking like a runaway incandescent red fire-hose of incredible electrical energy. When we allow our internal fires to burn and arise naturally within our chakras, or energy centers, we dissolve the blockages that obstruct the path to heightened awareness. With love and understanding, anyone can make sexuality a doorway to the Higher Self. We are Light, returning to Light, through our sexuality.

Woman Is the Bringer of Joy

Woman is the Bringer of Joy. Her crowning achievement is a state of consciousness that yogis call *"ananda,"* Love-Bliss-Absolute. This Joy is not an emotion but a natural condition of being. It is a sacred gift that lies within the heart of everyone who focuses in the moment.

Happiness and pleasure are outer reflections. Joy is a grounded state where we return to get our fulfillment. Happiness leads to giddiness; joy leads to bliss. By awakening joy we kindle our Divine nature. Use love as an instrument to revive your oneness with the Divine. Bliss is your Goddess nature. It is not a goal or destination but something that you are now.

The Divine Goddess exists within you. All you have to do is remember Her--well, almost all. Psyche's story will show you the permanent way to joy.

18

In the wonderful story of Psyche and Eros we have the full-fledged journey of the soul.

Jean Houston

Psyche and Eros

The myth of Psyche and Eros reveals the wisdom of love in the work of soulmaking. It teaches us that the wholeness we seek in someone or something else paradoxically can be obtained only from within our own being. To understand the adventure of a female nature striving for wholeness, explore the story:

There was once a king who had three daughters. The youngest daughter, Psyche, was so beautiful that her fame spread far and wide. People would travel great distances just to gaze upon her. Everyone offered her the admiration and adoration they would give a goddess. The people even called her the "New Aphrodite."

When her two sisters were grown they both married splendid kings, but poor Psyche, with all her beauty, remained alone and sad. Her state of perfection was so great that she was always worshiped but never courted. She began to hate her beauty because it only seemed to cause her loneliness.

Seeing her plight, her father traveled to Apollo's Oracle to ask how a suitable husband might be found. The Oracle instructed him to leave Psyche upon a great rock, dressed in funeral clothes, and her predestined husband would make her his wife. With great sadness, she was tied to a rock on the mountain and left there to become the Bride of Death. In terror, Psyche awaited her cruel fate.

It is dangerous to make the god/ess jealous, even unintentionally. The reputation of Psyche's beauty had spread far and wide, which made Aphrodite feel neglected and more than just a little jealous. A mere mortal was getting all the attention; attention Aphrodite felt should have been reserved for her alone. Vengefully, she asked her son, Eros, to use the power of his arrows, from which there was no defense, to pierce Psyche's heart and enchant her into falling in love with some despicable creature.

At his mother's bidding, Eros went forth to "do the dastardly deed." But when he saw her helplessly chained to a rock, he felt as though he had pricked himself with his own arrow. He instantly fell in love with her. He said nothing to his mother, but with the help of the winds, ferried her to a secret mansion that had been built for a god. Psyche became the Bride of Love. Through voices in her ears, Psyche was told that this paradise was hers, provided by her husband. She would have all she desired by day and the company of world's greatest lover only at night. She was never to look upon her husband nor to ask about his ways, or else they would be separated forever. She agreed.

Psyche's paradise was a majestic kingdom. It was a place without people, where she was attended by invisible servants. In time, Psyche grew bored with her lonely paradise and wanted to see her sisters. She implored Eros, saying, "I cannot see you and now I can't even see my own sisters. I shall die of isolation. Please let me see them." Unable to see her so sad, Eros consented but warned her not to talk about him or the things he had provided her, for that would be dangerous.

When Psyche saw her sisters, she forgot Eros' warning and told her sisters about the grandeur of her home and her incredibly romantic lover. Predictably, her sisters were envious and tried to persuade Psyche to tell them the identity of her husband. Psyche described him, attempting to appease them, but her stories conflicted. Her sisters, soon convinced her she had married a demon. Why else would she not be allowed to look at him? They told her to hide a sharp knife and a lamp beside the bed, and when he went to sleep, to light the lamp and stab him.

Psyche agreed. But when she lit the lamp and saw a magnificent god sleeping so peacefully in her bed, she was smitten by his beauty and began shaking. In her anxious excitement to explore him, she accidentally pricked herself with one of his arrows and fell deeply in love with him. Nearly swooning, she dropped the knife and spilled some oil from the lamp upon the sleeping Eros. Awakened by the sting of burning oil, he arose without a word and flew home to his mother.

Already pregnant with his child, Psyche was determined to spend the rest of her life, if necessary, trying to bring him back. She prayed to all the god/ess but none would help her for fear of Aphrodite's wrath. Finally, she went to Aphrodite and offered herself as a servant. Aphrodite quickly acquiesced and vented her anger upon Psyche by commanding her to perform a series of seemingly impossible tasks.

Psyche's first task was to separate a vast quantity of small mixed seeds into piles of each individual type. Worst of all, she had to complete this task before nightfall. Overwhelmed by a task that appeared totally impossible, Psyche dropped to her knees and began to cry. The ants of the field came to her rescue and, in no time, divided the great pile into lesser piles of perfect order.

The second task was to fetch some golden fleece from a herd of dangerous wild rams. Again overcome by grief, she sank into a pit of despair. How could she do such a thing and live to tell of it? She was far too small, too frail, too. . .she would surely be killed. The river reeds befriended her and advised her to wait until night, when the rams would come to the river to drink. The rams had to push through a hedge of hanging briar bushes that grew along the way to the river. Psyche could wait there and collect the wool that became entangled in the thorns.

Aphrodite was surprised by Psyche's success and assigned her a more difficult task. Next, Psyche was told to fetch a crystal goblet full of water from the

River Styx. The Styx was a treacherous circular river that flowed from a high mountain peak into the bowels of the underworld. No mortal could touch its waters without being swept away by them. This time an eagle came to her aid. It flew to the river, swooped down and filled the goblet without touching the water.

Psyche's final task was the most difficult of all. This time she had to journey into the underworld. There she was to persuade Persephone to give her a box filled with beauty ointment that she must return to Aphrodite. At the opening to the underworld, she was aided by a magical tower that gave her explicit instructions, which she was warned to follow unfailingly. She was to say "No" many times. She was to refuse to help a lame donkey driver, a dying man, and three women who were weaving the threads of fate. She was also instructed not to eat much when she was in the underworld. Psyche followed the instructions to the letter and returned with the magical ointment.

Having successfully completed her last task, she knew she would soon reunite with her beloved and wanted to be as beautiful as the god to whom she was married, so she yielded to temptation and decided to apply a little ointment to her-self. As she opened the small box, she found that its magic did not create beauty. Instead, it was filled with a heavy sleeping potion that quickly overtook her.

This time it was Eros who came to her rescue. He went to the king of the god/ess and requested to be officially married and to make Psyche a goddess. This pleased Aphrodite, too. If Psyche was a goddess, she would be a suitable wife for her son and no longer a threat to her. So, with heaven in accord, they married, and from their union a child called Pleasure (or Joy) was born.

The Soul's Urge for Love

This story reveals the soul's initiation--the collective image of what is needed for psychological growth. By depicting the labors of womanhood, Psyche gives the clues to develop the feminine in both men and women. Told and retold, the tale unfolds on many levels. Jean Houston's book, *The Search for the Beloved*, and Robert Johnson's *She* are but two books that have explored it in detail. Psyche's birth brought "heaven's dew" falling to the earth. This myth is an allegory of spirit infusing the soul, and is a critical epic of human consciousness.

The Greek word psyche (the soul) means butterfly. It is a creature that goes through a metamorphosis and cocoon process before an awakening transformation. Psyche was a wounded child who needed love and relationships. Often feeling helpless and abandoned, she learned to awaken her joy and unite with her Eros.

The psyche is all our mental components, both conscious and unconscious, that give direction to our instinctive drives. The soul needs eros (physical, erotic love) for expression in the world. Each is the goal of the other, for their union is creative; they complete each other. Eros provides the fire that gives the soul its yearnings and the impetus to grow.

Eros is a raw regenerative spirit that longs for creative union. Although eros most commonly appears in the form of sexuality, it is generated by any forces that connect the personal to the beyond to create something new, such as creativity and spirituality. This magical essence is love, the great transformer, which is considered the foundation of both healing and learning. It is love alone that transmutes humanity's baser elements into higher, more creative states. It is through love that we ultimately develop our highest potential, stimulate evolutionary growth, and actualize our creative vision. When eros is present, we connect with a catalyst for change, and all relationships become mutually transformative, empowering, and challenging.

If you have energy, you have eros. **Where do you channel your erotic force?** Is it into your work? Do you dissipate this precious energy in dealing with your "beast," scattering it through frivolity and glamour? Without eros in some form, creativity suffers. Without the lure to become, you do not develop. Without the yearning for the Beloved Goddess, you cannot find unity.

I am blessed with an erotic love relationship with my work, with my partner, and with the Beloved. All these relationships are fertile and transformative. It is the eros of my devotional nature that pulls me along the path.

Eros in my creative work feels like being in love. Writing for me is intense erotic involvement--I merge with it. I live each passage and each goddess intensely. I hope this book is also an erotic experience for you. It is erotic if it's an absorbing interaction that stimulates thought, heightens awareness, and fosters discovery.

The mythical Eros was Aphrodite's son and constant companion. Also called Amour and Cupid, he was associated with fire and death, because he had the ability to destroy as well as to create. His arrows were like a phallus: they pierced and fertilized the arid earth, making it produce lush green growth.

In the story, Psyche's sisters accused Eros of being a demon, but in actuality he was a "diamon." Rollo May in *Love and Will* defines the diamonic as, "Any natural function that has power to take over the whole person." Think of the diamonic Eros, not as an entity but, as an archetypical function of human experience. The diamonic is a creative and destructive force that either ennobles or degrades us. Sex, anger, rage, and the craving for power are examples. Yet, as Rilke wrote, "If my devils are to leave me, I am afraid my angels will take flight as well." The opposite of the diamonic is the death urge--apathy and the instinct to withdraw.

Eliminating the Female Sacrifice

Like Psyche, too many women suffer from being "too much." *Have you ever been asked to make sacrifices because you had too much energy, had too much beauty, or were too smart?* How often have you tried to "shrink to fit?" Do you ever sacrifice your potential so as not to arouse jealousies or confront negative feelings in yourself and others? Many women suppress their female power and natural talents in the pursuit of love.

A classic example came from Bonny, a client who talked about the pain she felt when her friends turned from her after she had won a beauty contest at the age of seventeen. This experience seemed to teach her that to succeed meant to lose love. When I was younger, I believed that if I shined too brightly I would cast shadows on others. I chose to appear less than I was, feeling that others would like me more.

Women sometimes feel a competitiveness toward each other. Often, people unconsciously feel that another person's success mirrors their own worthlessness. *Do you ever automatically act from this social conditioning and prevent others from achieving something "for their own good"?* In college during rush, I remember some of my sorority sisters strongly criticizing beautiful, dynamic women; yet more average women passed their analysis with ease. *Do you ever feel jealous of others who are doing better than you?* If so, don't envy anyone for anything! Jealousy and envy block your ability to advance spiritually. Remember, lakes freeze but freely flowing rivers do not.

How openly do you acknowledge the strengths and virtues of others? Are you afraid it will go to their heads? Do you want to guard your feelings? Are you embarrassed to openly acknowledge the accomplishments of another? If you cannot openly appreciate others, you probably can't appreciate yourself either. Start now by saying to yourself, "I take joy in all that you are and all that you do, but it's great to be me."

Psyche's wedding was celebrated as if it were a funeral. Being tied to the mountain of death ended Psyche's childhood naivete. After all, marriage is the death of maidenhood. We must grow up and sacrifice our innocence to become a part of a loving couple.

The spiritual journey implies coming to terms with feelings of loss and the inevitability of death. Everyone bears a wound through which the soul can develop. We need to heal our wounds and learn to be emotionally secure to manifest power in our own right.

In Psyche's marriage, she was first dominated by her male and was not allowed to ask for consciousness. Many women experience their masculine energy only through the men in their lives. To evolve, these women must break the unconscious patterns of domination that men impose upon them. When a woman fails to develop her male side, she lacks force of will and is easily controlled. The reverse is equally true of men. Jung said that the anima and animus function most effectively as mediators between the conscious and unconscious parts of the personality. Eros, Psyche's animus, does not want the responsibility of a conscious relationship. Still bound to his mother, he needs first to be psychologically weaned.

Psyche's passage with Eros through the unconscious was an adventure into an imaginative and creative world. Her paradise wasn't a place that fit on a map, but it existed for her all the same. The rapture of Eros enabled her to do the impossible, but she was warned of the dangers of talking about these things.

When I began my study of the intuitive sciences, I was enraptured with my private world--a safe haven populated by symbols, lists, and facts. But like Psyche, I quickly learned that I could not discuss these things with others. I did not yet know their essence, for my right brain did not always let the left brain know what it was doing. For a while it was acceptable to live in darkness; it nurtured and seeded me. But, the time came to leave the realm of darkness, or else spiritual growth would be arrested.

A Need for A Sisterhood

Psyche's sisters married patriarchal kings from the real world. They represent the material aspect of life. The sisters symbolize the raging voices within and without who demand that we "come to consciousness." Their words transformed Psyche from a naive self-satisfied child into a more conscious, loving individual. Their jealousy was aroused because Psyche advanced beyond their station.

Our sisters are our women friends who reflect our progress and serve as our shadows and our helpers and way-showers. Although they will challenge and envy us and may even be cruel, they push us toward the way of the soul. When a friend says something that irritates you, look within, for you too have that voice inside you, otherwise it would not bother you so much.

Let yourself have your friends, for through them you gain strength--emotional, mental, and spiritual support. Angeles Arrien told me, "Women tend to support each other emotionally, but not professionally; whereas men tend to support each other professionally, but not emotionally." Join with other kindred spirits and actively help them emotionally as well as professionally. As we draw together with our sisters in support groups, we can act as catalysts to bring each other out of darkness.

Seeking Light and Discrimination

Psyche's sisters advised her to bring a lamp and a knife to her bed. The knife, a male symbol, represents both destruction and discrimination. It is used to sever the veil of illusion but should never be turned upon others, such as with cutting sarcasm or biting words.

The lamp is a source of light in the darkness. Houston says that throughout history, the presence of women has been the "lamp of remembrance for men." Johnson says a man finds meaning in life and gathers self-esteem from his anima. When a man is discouraged, it is only his woman within who can restore his sense of value. There is a primal hunger within men to be near the light of a female partner and to acknowledge that light within. As we awaken the Light of our Goddess, we are no longer dominated by our inner partner--our animus or anima.

After Psyche broke the taboo of Eros' invisibility and saw her handsome god, she was no longer an infatuated maiden. Now, she was an erotic woman in love who wanted to know all about the incredible being whom she had married. In her desire to examine him more closely, she burned him. Oil was Psyche's means of light or understanding. Houston says oil is feminine, for it is the essence of the plant world. It burned Eros, which put an end to Psyche's pleasant but unconscious lifestyle. Men are afraid to be burned by the light of feminine seeing.

Eros, having been seen in his natural form, then had to leave his beloved Psyche. He could not help her yet. Even if the soul receives the illuminating fire of erotic passion, it must be tempered and trained before it can safely awaken. Psyche must face her "Dark Night of the Soul" before she unites with her divine connection. Alone, pregnant, fearful, and often suicidal, Psyche was overwhelmed by her problems until she learned to surrender to the process and wait for the remedy to arrive. The spiritual path brings phases of struggle, dryness, and doubt; it is all part of the process. There is no failure as long as we continue to make an effort.

My Dark Night of the Soul came during my fifth year of counseling. I had to overcome my fear of not making it in the world. For several months I experienced considerable negative support from the universe. Within a day my newspaper column, and access to my neighbor's computer were taken from me. Then I had to endure a five-day bout with the flu and soaring temperatures. After that came critical feedback from my teachers and my family, who were not sparing in their advice--"Get another job." Nothing seemed to be working, not even getting my hair permed during this period, for it came out frizzy. Feeling ugly, fearful, and abandoned, I felt as though I were moving slowly through the darkness. I was traveling through a dark tunnel, but if I focused, I could see a light at the end. I fixed my attention on the light and eventually I was out. I realized My Dark Night of the Soul's purpose was purification, to strip away all remnants of my old selves, in order to build a new me. Only when I admitted that I would sacrifice all for my eros (work) was I relieved from the fear. Now, I just do my work and the support takes care of itself.

Focus on the Light in those Dark Places

Remember, the light of the Sun is always shining behind those clouds. Surrender to the Goddess to raise your consciousness above the dense storm clouds of life. You cannot always see the light, but know that, as on a cloudy day, the sun rises. Just wait and the constructive avenues of opportunity will become apparent.

This myth teaches us to appeal to the very god/ess within who are wounding us and to ask them for relief. Aphrodite, by her competitive and critical nature, does what is necessary to make Psyche grow. The tasks chosen portray the innate abilities of the female nature that need to be made conscious.

Trusting Inner Allies

Psyche's first ordeal of sorting the seeds was solved by ants. This task seemed impossible, but in reality it was small. By learning to follow our own instinctual natures, each of us can effortlessly sort out life's petty problems, one at a time, not all at once. Like Psyche, we learn not to give up but to give over. Our task is to connect with the instinctual order that lies within our inner resources.

We need to set priorities and discriminate between our conflicting feelings and competing subpersonalities. We must also separate our personal world from that of the collective. These labors, which every warrior must face, require an inward turning of awareness. Only within ourselves can we systematically sort through our shifting motives and values. Only within the psyche can we separate our fleeting, externally generated desires from the truly important needs that empower our souls.

Finding Noncompetitive Methods

Psyche was instructed, as her second task, to capture the power of the great ram by taking its wool. The ram is a symbol of the competitive world, which is full of dangerous masculine energies. Its fleece represents wealth and power. The advice of the singing reeds was to avoid direct contact with the rams. Retrieve the wool left behind in the bushes, at night while the rams rested.

The reeds rising from the water represent the wisdom of growth and its sense of timing. The reeds are those parts of us that tap into our intuitive knowledge, which knows that all is possible through cooperation.

Psyche succeeded by understanding the "nature of the beast" and by using feminine wisdom. She also learned to be content by gathering just enough fleece. To wield power without being destroyed by it, we need to learn truthful, compassionate, coop-erative methods that eliminate the struggle for power. To get what we want without losing our inner peace, we should pursue our needs and desires in ways that avoid destructive confrontations with others. We can learn to use networking as an art of working together and sharing cooperatively.

Acquiring Presence and Mindfulness

Psyche was asked to fetch a glass of water from the River Styx, which is the symbol of the waters of life. The Styx flows from the highest to the lowest levels of the underworld and is guarded by fierce dragons. Like Psyche, we have to face the dragons that lurk at the threshold of life.

Our dragons are those repetitive habits that keep us preoccupied and too busy to concentrate. They can be the family, the job, the government, society, or our own personal darkness inside. Dragons don't give us much respect until we follow the path, for only then do we access the waters of life. If we do not, we eventually turn into one of those attendant dragons, hanging on the mountain near the Styx. This task may appear like a monumental feat, but as the myth again tells us, help is always present.

Zeus sent Psyche a high flying eagle with panoramic vision. The eagle symbolizes the perceptions of the Higher Mind, which are available to all with an eye to see. By learning to gain some emotional distance, we can see the overall patterns of our lives. By this act we are told to fill ourselves by fetching this water of life safely from the air, not the earth--from the mind, not the senses. With the help of our animus and a penetrating vision, we can then relate to life in all its vastness and enjoy all its many possibilities.

The crystal goblet symbolizes the frailty of the ego, which must be handled delicately. Like a pure crystal, the ego takes on the "color" of anything with which it comes in contact. The feminine way is to take one goblet at a time, in essence to do one thing at time and do it well--to concentrate and **Be Here Now**.

Exploring the Underworld

Psyche's journey into the underworld (the unconscious) was her most perilous test. We cannot have transformation without the inner journey as a prerequisite. This journey is often painful, frustrating, and confusing and it never progresses without some sacrifice. All the hidden darkness must be brought to the surface and faced, cleansed, and changed.

Our darkness is spun out of our less conscious emotions, including those we share with the collective. Like Psyche, we must go into the darkness, for there is wisdom to be found if we follow our feelings to their source. Like the old alchemical quote says, "For a tree's branches to reach into heaven, its roots must penetrate into hell."

Many people will resist letting go and living from their bowels. Plunge into your depths and experience your life. You have to feel those old pains to heal them. Being receptive is not enough. Take heed from Psyche's trials and know you do not have to complete your tasks alone. Much like hiring a guide to tour the wilderness, it is wise to make the trip with someone, like a therapist, who has gone there before and knows a safe approach.

Psyche received her final instructions from the Tower, a phallic symbol. The tower is an ally and stands for any wisdom or culture with its logic and discipline, such as our traditions, religions, and philosophical systems. However to some people, their tower is a tower of Babel, made from their belief systems, individual rules, conditioning and peer pressure. *What is the dominant tower in your life?* Yoga, mythology, astrology, tarot, I Ching and the Qabalah are my stable anchors that allow me to soar and still be grounded.

Learning to Say, "No"

The tower warned Psyche, in essence, to limit her availability to others. She was told not to eat much in the underworld, for "when one eats, one is somehow committed." You need to watch for runaway urges that carry you toward over-consumption or excessive generosity. Either will bind you to your "underworld."

Psyche was not to help the dying man or the lame donkey driver to pick up his sticks. We must say, "No" compassionately to the voices of those who would arouse our emotions. Wants, whether ours or someone else's, are not demands. Although we may regard other's desires as imperatives, they are only requests, subject to our approval. Admittedly, some requests are more forceful than others, but we are not here just to fulfill the personal desires of another. Kindness and giving are curious virtues. People may present us with an endless stream of reasons why their "needs" are genuine, but it isn't always wise to help others by continually pandering to the desires created by their personalities.

Say, "No" to thoughtless and inappropriate requests, to anything that violates your standards, or to what other people should do for themselves. Saying, "No" is often a difficult but necessary human right, for you need to set goals and keep them when others are pleading or nagging you. Say, "No" quickly to prevent false expectations being raised. Although you do not have to justify every refusal, offer a counter proposal when making a difficult refusal.

As a Goddess Warrior, you need discrimination, especially with relationships that allow negativity to enter your sphere of influence. I have had to refuse to listen to friends' "sad tales of woe" because, in a nonprofessional environment, they were negatively affecting me. Friendships are not open obligations to share "war stories." Remember, you always have a choice! Do not allow yourself to be unduly imposed upon. Watch that you are not diverted from doing your real work because of desires or demands from others. In primitive societies, when a person did things for another, it caused indebtedness. It is no different today.

Psyche was told to say, "No" to the three women who were the weavers of fate, which means we must resist the temptation to know or influence the fate of others. Fate making is a seduction, particularly for psychics and counselors in the helping professions and for those mothers whose tendency is to give up their lives for their children.

Overcoming Collective Glamour

Psyche failed her next trial because curiosity and vanity weakened her resolve. Psyche was a real beauty. She did not need what was in the box; it was only her vanity that made her think she did. Todays woman is under a great deal of pressure to look good; she spends a lot of time and money on her body and appearance. My personal feeling is that a degree of controlled vanity helps serve the Goddess, for a pleasant appearance gives one a feeling of confidence. A sense of aesthetics can inspire us to stay fit and maintain a high level of self-esteem. In fact, many people start by perfecting their outer appearances and then move on to work on their inner natures.

Persephone's beauty box, however, symbolizes the collective glamour of Maya. Glamour can be a seduction that operates through universal feelings and trends and pulls us into the ecstatic spell of collective thought. Her web is woven from the gilded threads of our own desires. Glamour's power sometimes captivates the will, entrances the mind, and overwhelms our desire for self-rule. The price we pay for this bonding is the loss of individuality. We can see Maya in the world of fashion, where, like chameleons, many women get swept into her dictates.

The way of the Goddess Warrior is to find our very own sense of beauty and break the collective habit of always going "outer." We eventually learn that, as a Goddess, the outer really doesn't matter. We shine with light from within, not from glitter on the outside.

In spite of Psyche's mindfulness, her desire to be more beautiful for her lover made her disobey her tower. She bent the rules by opening the box, which condemned her to the "sleep of death." Similarly, we go unconscious when we neglect to follow our personal disciplines and when the Watcher is asleep. Slipping into unconsciousness represents those old patterns we have worked on and thought we were rid of, but that inadvertently reappear. Often the reappearance of hidden flaws is an opportunity for growth.

Psyche's error was necessary for her to grow and complete herself. We too, can learn so much from our mistakes if we try. Psyche's sleep was the psychological death necessary for transformation, which prepared her for the grace of being a Goddess. We too have to go through a gestation period before opening our joyous nature.

The Sacred Marriage

Psyche fell prey to an old habit. But, because she had developed her latent abilities, gathered some male power, fetched the essence of the water of life, explored her underworld, and was willing to sacrifice all to be with her love, she was saved by Eros.

Eros, like the powers of nature, could come only at the right time--only after he matured from a wounded boy into a manly savior. For our eros to endure, it must be mirrored and understood through the soul over time. Love without the soul is empty and vain. The spirit of eros deepens from the exchanges of human experience, just as the soul gains from the richness of the archetypical world.

Psyche and Eros were at last united with the consent of all the god/ess--an act of humanity and transformation transcending everyday reality. Psyche's salvation was the gift of the Goddess that accompanied the union of love with the soul. The promise of co-creation is in the act of Becoming. Besides, it was impossible to imprison love, especially after discovering instinct, some male power, light, discrimination, presence, inaccessibility, and wisdom.

The crowning glory of this story was Pleasure, or Joy, the daughter. The child's Greek name was *Voluptia,* which means "plunging into life." When we learn to be in full possession of our Goddess, we plunge into life, which is transformed into a dance of pure joy.

19

Wholeness and Integration

The boon of fulfilling the "labors of Psyche" is wholeness or integration. The sacred marriage happens in every moment by acknowledging emotions and intuitions and blending them with words and actions. We invoke female power by being present and by focusing intensely on whatever we do. Only by giving every task our full and undivided attention can we manifest the force needed to succeed. The clues that guide us from one task to the next are unearthed through this mental focus. Focus allows integration.

The way of the Goddess Warrior is to learn to operate from a high degree of inner strength and trust in the process, no matter what the details look like in the moment. You develop complete trust in your own appropriateness, with a firm commitment to act from your inner nature. This is your Goddess energy. Always trust what comes from your own inner truth. You will know your truth when you harmonize your heart with your head. When you balance your female and male energies, you truly become centered--having peaceful clarity within and joyous movement without, a union of strength and gentleness.

When we are in our power, we are not easily knocked from our center by outside influences. For example, intense desires seduce us off center; fears knock us off center; covert manipulation drags us off center; and addictions pull us off center.

In Summary

As the Tigress story showed us, making this sacred psychological journey demands that we embrace our true nature by fighting our past conditionings. The many parts of our personality must bind together with Spirit. As we learned in the tale of the Two Sisters, the golden thread of Spirit does not have the power to lift us unless the beast is well trained. Only then can we follow the whispers of the universe while serving biological life on earth.

Like the Well Frog, we must break out of our parochial world and leap through the void to experience Universal Consciousness. Only a life identified with the Goddess can bridge the abyss that separates Spirit from matter.

The Way of the Goddess Warrior is a path called by many names--Soulmaking, the Hero's Journey, the Great Adventure, the visionary quest, the Great Work, or the process of individuation. It is a journey toward self-knowledge, balance and Unity. The way of the Goddess Warrior is operating behind a shield of love and integrity, which means accepting yourself and others unconditionally and living with truth, fairness and harmlessness. The process fosters motivation, purpose, focus, awareness, practice, and nonattachment. All are needed to succeed. Our challenge is to wake up, be centered and invoke the Goddess.

WAKE UP means:

o   Awakening the feminine to bring balance to the world.

o   Choosing to live from the Light of your soul.

o   Motivating your Virginal self to set goals.

o   Exploring your personal myth, your sacred wound and your unconscious, so you can quiet the inner subpersonalities and live within the Grand Myth.

o   Wakening consciousness by finding dynamic presence--Being Here Now.

o   Acquiring discrimination, by combating condition-
      ings and the unseen forces of Maya.

o   Instilling ethical perfection, by abandoning any
      unethical modes of living.

o   Developing an enlightened will. Asking for what you
      want, despite appearances, but being unattached to
      the outcome.

o   Making choices, by following your inner motivations,
      and taking daily action.

BE CENTERED implies:

o   Finding your spiritual Source.

o   Taming the beast or lower nature.

o   Balancing and integrating the male and female
      within.

o   Maintaining inner peace by practicing meditation
      and surrendering to the process.

INVOKE THE GODDESS includes:

o   Seeking your Light by learning Holy Theurgy, the art
      of putting on a god-form.

o   Connecting with your archetypical heredity.

o   Releasing who you think you are and opening to the
      greater Unity of who you really are.

o   Trusting your intuitive powers to lead the process,
      by acting "from the inside out."

o   Transcending the past by healing your own Inner
      Child

o   Acquiring self-love and becoming your own
      Caretaker.

o   Choosing wisely whether or not to be a mother

o   Living with your womanly wonders--being loving,
      appreciative, creative, erotic and joyful.

o   Mastering the "labors of Psyche" which means:

o   Eliminating the feminine sacrifice,

o   Seeking a sisterhood, light, and discrimination,

o   Trusting your instincts,

o   Finding noncompetitive methods,

o   Acquiring presence,

o   Exploring the underworld,

o   Learning to say, "No," and

o   Overcoming vanity and unconsciousness.

o   Since the Goddess encompasses the invisible
     support of the universe, it also includes networking
     or joining with like-minded others who are
     sympathetic to your cause.

Grounding the Goddess

There must be imagination if there is to be hope.
Everyone needs a personal image of the Great Goddess.
*Try drawing the many faces of the Goddess, as part
of your process.* Even if you think you can't, do it
anyway--for the process will awaken your latent creativity.
These active visions will greatly enhance your growth process.

*Visualize yourself as the Goddess, in touch
with your female power.* Close your eyes now, and
imagine what your future self will be like. How does
that image differ from what you are now? What must
you do to truly become your own hero?

Remember that the essence of being a Goddess is love.
Love the "present you," not just the "you-that-will-be"
after you lose those extra pounds or reach enlightenment.
Only when you accept yourself as you are now do you
give yourself permission to grow.

*To find your personal image, it is important
that you know both your strengths and your weaknesses.* Pull the pieces of your subpersonalities
together and let the archetypical information presented
in this book guide you. Tap into your own special
counselors, those archetypical selves that are alive and
well within you. Visualize those inner loving friends
who have mastered your challenges and are there to
guide and nurture you to find solutions to problems.

If you do, the picture of your own essence will begin to appear. When you recognize which of the goddesses govern you, your personal myth will come to life. You will be able to see new role models that will naturally change your personality to be more connected with the Divine Goddess of your soul.

The Goddess' way is to trust the natural process of unfolding and gain. Her measure is unconditional love, a compassionate force that never lapses. Identify with her greatest boon, inner joy, and her truest gift, bliss. Accept her blessings, guidance and magic.

To embody this image, you must live as a Goddess. Simply memorizing all the glib words is not enough. Remember, "The steps to getting there are being there." "Fake it before you make it." "Identification is the master key."

Focus on feeling the Goddess deeply. Let her nature envelope you. See yourself as a Child of Light, a Goddess caring for the human family that is happily growing. Envision yourself on the quest and, in each moment, choose to focus on your Goddess qualities--love, peace, compassion, trust, joy, and so on.

It all starts by accepting your greatness and committing to your dreams in total love. Learn to trust yourself and your own knowingness so that you can live each moment telling your truth and sharing your feelings and thoughts. Daydream and let yourself have your heart's desire. Tap into the gentle influence of the Goddess and seek the tranquility of the spirit.

Awakening Soul Power

Awakening female power means transforming your personality into a Being of Light. The secret to infusing life with the power of the soul lies in having a heart filled with trust. When we arouse the Goddess with bhakti (devotion and spiritual love) and seek answers from our center, trust naturally awakens. Trusting means having an unshakable faith in the divine order of the universe. Faith breaks the illusion of separateness and love accelerates evolution toward unity with Universal Consciousness. Learn to live by attaching yourself to the spiritual light. The light of Divine Consciousness shines within

everyone to dispel ignorance and darkness. We are all
moving toward the realization of the Divine Mother (or
whatever your chosen ideal of God) and will arrive sooner
or later, the only question is when. The most expedient
way is through love.

With love we let our radiant inner being shine and see
the awe-inspiring goodness of our Higher Self. Love never
diminishes, for the more we give away the more there is.
Beam love out from your heart as if you were made of
pure light, for in truth you are. Glow radiantly! Let your
brilliance dissolve all obstructions. Try staying in love
whether you have a partner or not: be in love with yourself and your Source.

As Goddess Warriors we are asked to walk alone and,
bit by bit, to draw every aspect of our vast diversity into a
single whole being. Only after we have thoroughly
explored our inner nature can we quiet the many voices
within.   Only then, can our many subpersonalities be
molded into one synergistic superset--the Master Personality.

We find this Master Personality when our Watcher is
awake in every moment. Through the Watcher, we
experience our emotions with no more intensity than we
feel a breeze. We know its temperature and the direction
from which it came, but we are not affected by it. As we
embrace wholeness, and are firmly rooted in the Goddess,
events come and go, but we are in charge. Then the distinctions between the executive personality and all other
separate subpersonalities, begin to break down. The result
of this alchemical amalgamation is an enlightened consciousness.

All who finish will know that "The treasure you seek is
within you." A Hindu story told by Sri Ramakrishna illustrates this point:

There was once a very poor woman who went to the
forest every day to gather wood. It was work that
barely kept her alive, but it was all she could do. One
day she met with a holy man who took pity on her and
solemnly advised her to "go deeper." She did not
understand the instructions, but the next day she
traveled farther into the forest than she had ever gone
before. To her delight she found some valuable sandalwood trees, which would bring her a good price. At first

she was overjoyed, but after reflecting awhile, she felt she was not to stop there. She left the sandalwood and journeyed deeper into the forest until she came to a stream. There, while drinking, she noticed something shimmering in the water. She had found a silver mine. But again, she remembered the words of the holy man, "Go deeper." So she continued onward. No sooner had she left the silver behind than she come across a gold mine. Still she heard the voice saying, "Go deeper." Although reluctant to leave this great wealth, she moved beyond. Deeper still, she came upon a diamond mine, and there she knew she had found her prize. She contentedly rested with her "pearl of great price."

This parable reminds us to go deeper into our personalities, for therein lies great wealth. Do not be tempted to stop as you acquire the boons of the different goddesses and metaphysical systems, but continue to go deeper until you truly find the great riches of your Divine nature. Don't stop until you have the diamond-like strength of the Philosopher's Stone--reach God realization.

We all create our own gods, but paradoxically, the ultimate letting go is to release all those created beings and merge with the Higher Self within. My process was to stop praying to God the Father outside, to eliminate creating with magic, to inhibit the practice of psychic prediction, and to forego channeling a spirit guide. Each stage of learning nurtured me along the way, but the real jewel came when I began to feel the Divine Mother moving within.

The key that opens the door to the Inner Sanctum is total identification with the Higher Self or Goddess. It is only found by going inside and trusting your connection with the Source. You must learn to "roll away the stone" and resurrect the Goddess from her prison of matter.

Meditate on Unity as your tiniest point within-your point of bliss--and feel its power. The Goddess is All That Is, and All That Is, is Love. Do not look outside yourself or give your power to others. Say, "I am one with Divine Creation; I am one with the Goddess."

By choosing light for yourself, you will aid all others to realize their fullest potential. See the Divine in everyone. Only by becoming your sister's and brother's helper can you heal yourself and subsequently the planet.

In Loving Conclusion

Through the seven years that I have been writing this book, I have been bonding with you, my reader, in compassion and love. If my process has served you, please write to me and let me know. We would love to hear from you and share our newsletter--The SoulSource Resource.

Now that you have finished this book, I firmly recommend that you go back over it, answer the questions, and do the processes. Keep a journal. It is an extremely effective way to express your feelings and communicate with your Goddess.

Share this book with your friends and join with others who are sympathetic to your cause. Maybe you feel inclined to initiate a support group to encourage female power, awaken your courageous Warrior, and celebrate your Goddess. We all naturally have the frailty of sloth and need to help each other work on ourselves.

Let us help each other--to wake up, embrace our inner partners, and share ourselves, our talents, and our abilities in ways that are free of repression. Let us support each other--to shine, express, and participate! If we link our minds and form a sisterhood of trust, we can recreate the Earth as a place where all its parts can be supported and nurtured. Only then can we become trustworthy stewards of our planetary future and take our rightful place in evolution.

As I continue my heroic adventure, working toward enlightenment, I am learning to "walk the talk." I continually remind myself to be patient and persistent and to dare. Following my dreams means bringing them to form, step-by-step. My daily challenge is to stay conscious and keep "my head in the heavens, but my feet on the ground." Being a practical optimist, I know there is hope, but that it takes work. Since the process is the goal, each moment is the doorway to opportunity.

My deepest wish for you, fellow traveler, is to awaken your female power, for when you do, you celebrate your Goddess and co-create with the Divine. It is the road to being the best that you can be! Furthermore, as you grow, we all grow. May the Goddess bless you.

A List of Stories, Processes, Metaphors, and Poems

Notes, Reference and Bibliography

Arrien, Angie, *The Tarot Handbook, Practical Applications of Ancient Visual Symbols*, Arcus Publishing Company, P.O. Box 228, Sonoma, CA, 95476, 1987.

Arroyo, Steven, *Astrology, Karma and Transformatio*, CRCS Publications, Sabastopol, CA, 95473, 1978.

Assagioli, Roberto, *Psychosynthesis*, An Esalen Book, Penguin Books, Ltd., England, 1965, p.88.

Bandler, Richard and John Grinder's *Reframing*, Real People Press, Box F, Moab, Utah, 1982.

Bennis, Warren and Burt Namus, *Leaders, The Strategies for Taking Care*, Harper and Row, New York, NY, 1985.

Blum, Ralph, *The Book Of Runes*, St. Martin's Press, 175 Fifth Ave., New York, NY, 10010, 1982.

Bly, Robert, audio tape entitled, *Fairy Tales For Men and Women*, Ally Press Center, 524 Orleans Street, St.Paul, MN, 55107, 1986.

Bolen, Jean, *Goddesses In Everywoman, A New Psychology of Women*, Harper and Row, 10 East 53rd St., New York, NY, 1984.

Bradshaw, John, *Homecoming , Reclaiming and Championing Your Inner Child* , Bantam Books, NY,1990.

Campbell, Joseph, *The Power Of Myth*, Doubleday, New York, 1988 and video series, especially p.18, 27, 125, 160, 201.

----*A Hero With A Thousand Faces* , Bollingen Series XVII, Princeton University Press, 1949.

----edited by Campbell, *The Portable Jung* , Viking Press, New York, 1971.

----*An Open Life, Joseph Campbell In Conversation With Micheal Toms* , edited by John M. Maher and Dennie Briggs, New Dimensions Foundation, 1988, p.35.

Cole-Whittaker, Terry, *Love and Power in a World without Limits: A Woman's Guide to the Goddess Within* , Harper and Row, San Francisco, CA, 1989.

Collins, Judy, the song "Daughters of Time," from the Sanity and Grace tape, Gold Castle Records, Inc. P.O. Box 2568, Hollywood, CA, 90078.

Cowan, Connell and Melvyn Kinder's *Smart Women, Foolish Choices* , Crown Publishers, New York, NY, 1985, p.8-9.

Diamond, Carlin, *Love It, Don't Label It*, Fifth Wave Press, San Rafael, 1986.

Douglas, Nik and Penny Slinger, *Sexual Secrets* , Destiny Books, New York, NY, 1979, especially p. 126.

Downing, Christine, *The Goddess, Mythological Images of the Feminine* , Crossroad, New York, 1984, p.190, 211, 208.

Eisler, Raine, *The Chalice and the Blade, Our History, Our Future,* Harper and Row, San Francisco, CA, 1987.

Emery, Gary, *Own Your Own Life* , New American Library, New York, NY, 1982.

Fadiman, James, *Unlimit Your Life, Setting and Getting Goals* , Celestial Arts, Berkeley, CA, 1989.

Feinstein, David and Stanley Krippner, *Personal Mythology, The Psychology of Your Evolving Self* , J. P. Tarcher, Los Angeles, CA, 1989.

Ferrucci, Piero, *What We May Be,* J. P. Tarcher, Los Angeles, CA, 1982.

Fox, Matthew, *The Illumination of Hildegard of Bingen* , Bear and Company, Santa Fe, NM, 1985, p.30.

----*Hildegard's Book of Divine Works* , Bear and Company, Santa Fe, NM, 1987, p.ix and p.xiii.

----"Toward a Spiritual Renaissance," an interview through *Common Boundary* Magazine, Chevy Chase, MD, July/August, 1990.

Gawain, Shakti, *Living In The Light* , Whatever Publishing, Mill Valley, CA, 1986.

George, Demetra, *Astroid Goddesses*, ACS Publications, Inc. PO Box 16430, San Diego, CA, 92116, 1986.

Gimbutas, Marija, *The Goddesses and Gods of Old Europe, Myths and Cult Images* , University of California Press, Berkeley and Los Angeles, CA, 1982.

-----*The Language of the Goddess*, Harper and Row, San Francisco, CA, 1989.

Grant, Micheal, *Myths of the Greeks and The Romans* , Mentor Books, New American Library, Ontario, Canada, 1962.

Graves, Robert, *The Greek Myths: 1*, Penguin Books, Ltd., Harmondsworth, Middlesex, England, 1955.

---Introduction by Graves, *New Larousse Encyclopedia Of Mythology* , The Hamlyn Publishing Group, London, 1959.

Gray, John, *Feelings First* , Heart Publishing Co., Santa Monica, CA, 1984.

Greene, Liz, *The Astrology of Fate* , Samuel Weiser, P.O. Box 612, York Beach, Maine, 03910, 1984.

----*The Outer Planet and Their Cycles, the Astrology of the Collective* , CRCS Publication, Sabastopol, CA, 95473, 1983.

Hamilton, Edith, *Mythlogy*, Mentor Books, New American Library of World Literature, Inc., NY, 1040.

Heider, John, *The Tao of Leadership*, Humanics New Age, Atlanta, GA, 1985.

Houston, Jean, *The Search For The Beloved*, *Journeys In Sacred Psychology*, J.P. Tarcher, Los Angeles, CA, 1987, specifically p.16-17, p.29, 104-5, 168.

-----*The Possible Human*, 1982, J.P. Tarcher Inc., Los Angeles.

Husain, Shahrukh, *Demons, Gods and Holy Men*, Schocken Books, New York, NY,1987.

Iglehart, Hallie, *Woman Spirit*, Harper and Row, San Francisco, CA, 1983.

Johnson, Robert, *She, Understanding Feminine Psychology* , Harper and Row, San Francisco, CA, 1976.

----*Inner Work, Using Dreams and Active Imagination for Personal Growth* , Harper and Row, San Francisco, CA, 1986.

----*Ecstasy, Understanding the Psychology of Joy*, Harper and Row, San Francisco, 1987.

Johnson, Spencer, *One Minute for Myself*, William Morrow and Company, Inc, New York, NY, 1985.

Jung, Carl, *Man and His Symbols*, A Windfall Book, Doubleday & Company, Garden City, New York, NY, 1964.

Keyes, Ken, *Handbook To Higher Consciousnes* , Living Love Center, Cornucopia Institute, St. Mary, Kentucky, 40063, 1972.

Lang, R. D., *Vital Lies, Simple Truths, The Psychology of Self-Deceptoin*, Simon & Schuster, Science News Book advertisement, 1985.

Luthman, Shirley Gehrke, *Collection 1979*, Metetabel and Company, 4340 Redwood Highway, Suite 307, San Rafael, CA, 1980.

----*Energy and Personal Power*, Mehetabel and Company, San Rafael, 1982.

May, Rollo, *Love and Will* , W. W. Norton & Company, New York, 1969, p. 122.

Metzger, Deena, "Re-Vamping the World: On the Return of the Holy Prostitute," *Utne Reader* , August/Sept. 1985, p.120-124.

Metzner, *Ralph Opening To Inner Light* , J.P. Tarcher, Los Angeles, 1986, and audio tape.

Mookerjee, Ajit, *Kali, The Feminine Force* , Destiny Books, Ally Press, 524 Orleans Street, St. Paul, MN. 55107, 1988.

Moss, Richard, *The I That Is We, Awakening to Higher Energies Through Unconditional Love*, Celestial Arts, Berkeley, CA, 1981.

Munford, John, *Ecstasy Trough Tantra* , Llewellyn Publications, St.Paul, Minnesota, 55164-0383, 1988.

Naisbitt, John and Patricia Aburdene, *Megatrends 2000, Ten Directions for the 1990's* , William Morrow and Co. Inc., New York, NY, 1990, p.216-240.

Needleman, Jacob, "Psychotherapy and The Sacred," *Parabola* Magazine #1, p.52-65, especially p.54. (Two Sister's Story)

Nikhilananda, Swami, The Gospel of Sri Ramakrishna, Vedanta Press, Vedanta Place, Hollywood, CA, 90068, 1946, especially p.232-233, 109.

Patanjali, *How to Know God,* Yoga Sutras, Vedanta Press, 1946 Vadanta Place, Hollywood, CA, 90068, 1953.

Peck, Scott, *The Roadless Traveled,* Simon and Schuster, New York, NY, 1978.

Perera, Sylvia Brinton, *Descent to the Goddess, A Way of Initiation for Women,* Inner City Books, Box 1271, Station Q, Toronto, Canada M4T 2P4, 1981.

PPS Video Documentaries, *Woman: Myth and Reality* , Bernice Sander's work with the Association of American Colleges discussed the handicaps of being a woman, 1986.

----Sexual Brain, Distinction of man and woman's brains research was conducted by Dr. Melissa Heinz from the UCLA Diagnostic Imaging Center.

Sadhu, Mouni, *Concentration, A Guide to Mental Mastery* , Melvin Powers, Wilshire Book Company, No. Hollywood, CA, 1959.

Satchidananda, Swami, *Science of Mind* Magazine, September 1983, especially p.8-10 and 71.

Smothermon, Ron, *Winning Through Enlightenment,* Context Publications, San Francisco, CA, 1980.

Unity's Daily Word, Unity Village, MO, 64065.

Walker, Barbara G., *The Woman's Encyclopedia of Myths and Secrets,* Harper and Row, San Francisco, 1983.

Wilhelm, Richard, *The I Ching or Book of Changes* , Bollingen Series XIX, Princeton University Press, Princeton, NJ, 1950.

Wing, R.L., *The I Ching Workbook,* Doubleday, New York, NY, 1979, p.12.

-----*The Tao of Power,* Doubleday, New York, NY, 1986.

Woodman, Marion, "The Conscious Feminine," *Common Boundary* Magazine, March/April 1989.

Glossary of Terms and God/ess

Alchemy Thought to be a physical process of transmuting lead into gold, but was actually an esoteric psychological study designed to transform the gross material nature of the alchemist into the golden radiance of wisdom.

Amour (Latin) Another name for Eros or Cupid, the God of Love.

Ananda (Sanskrit) Love/Bliss/Absolute.

Androgynous Having both male and female natures within.

Anima (Jungian) The woman within a man.

Animus (Jungian) The man within a woman.

Alpha-male A dominant or breeding male.

Aphrodite (Greek) The Goddess of Love, Beauty and Creativity; our womanly wonders or our feminine, magnetic creative aspects; also called Venus.

Apollo (Greek and Roman) The god who personified the spirit of the Sun.

Apollo's Oracle Tells the undisputed fortune and fates, meant to represent the unconscious knowing.

Astrology Ancient metaphysical language that shows our relationship to the heavens; an excellent nomenclature of the personality.

Aquarius Astrological air sign representing the New Age; signifies group consciousness; its symbol is the water bearer.

Archetypes (Jungian) Universal patterns; primary life-motivating forces, i.e., blueprints of who we are.

Ares (Greek) God of War and Aggression; also called Mars.

Artemis (Greek) Virgin Goddess of the Moon and the Hunt; also called Diana.

Athena (Greek) Virgin Goddess of Wisdom, War, Strategy and Handicrafts; also called Minerva.

Atman (Sanskrit) The Higher Self.

Bhakti (Sanskrit) An intense devotional love of God.

Beast Metaphor representing a collection of primitive human programs concerning survival, the avoidance of pain, and the pursuit of pleasure; our baser nature.

Bodhi (Sanskrit) The awakened consciousness, Buddhist term for the Watcher.

Ceres (Roman) Mother Goddess of Grain & Agriculture; also called Demeter.

Chakras (Sanskrit) Psychic energy centers within the body.

Collective Unconscious (Jungian) Describtion of the hidden and ever changing web of consciousness that binds everyone together.

Crone   The Wise Old Woman within who has the ability to see beyond the crossroads of life.

Corpus Callosum   The interconnecting ganglia that unite the two hemispheres of the brain.

Cronus (Greek) Earth God of Fertility, who represents the divine Father principle; also called Saturn.

Demeter (Greek) See Ceres.

Devi (Sanskrit) A Goddess or shining being.

Devotee A person who honors the Divine through devotional practices.

Diamon   The erotic force within that has the power to take over; both a creative and a destructive force of renewal.

Diana   (Roman) See Artemis.

Endymoin   Mythological lover of Selene, Moon Goddess, who received immortality on the condition that he remain asleep.

Enlightenment   State of fulfillment resulting from total loss of personal identity due to absorption into absolute unity.

Eros   A connective force, an inner fire, a yearning to grow and create something new; most often expressed in physical erotic love; god whose arrows inflicted wounds of love, also called Cupid. See Amour.

Esoteric   Unpublished inner teachings, closed to all but a few.

Exoteric Commonly published teachings for the masses.

Ethical Perfection Self-imposed integrity; an impeccable code of behavior.

Female Warrior   A woman who is on the spiritual quest.

Fate Making   Becoming a determining factor in the lives of others.

Gaia (Greek) Mother Earth.

Gawain   Wise and noble knight of King Arthur's round table.

Genetic Programming   Character traits that are hard-coded into everyone's DNA/genes.

Glamour   Collective forces that seduce us into merging with its nature; can be seen in music, fashions, movies and advertising; also called Maya.

God/ess   An abbreviation for gods and goddesses, pronounced "godz."

Goddess Powers The potencies of the inner nature, such as intuition and emotional support.

Goddess Warrior Any Adventurer who is striving for integration and who wants to awaken female power.

Grace A state of being that Christians call "divine providence." Special divine dispensation said to result from the practice of ethical perfection.

Great Work The Hermetic counterpart of the Hero's Journey, to which there are three keys; one unlocks the potency of the aspirant, another unlocks the tools needed to build the Kingdom, and the last unlocks the gate to the Kingdom itself.

Great Goddess The Divine Mother concept.

Great Destiny The universal plan. See Great Work.

Greening Power Lush creativity of spring; God's freshness that humans receive through life force; the ability to create.

Grounded Term that means you are connected to your body, your environment and to your own truth.

Guru (Sanskrit) Dispeller of darkness. Spiritual master who possesses the "ear-spoken teachings."

Hatha Yoga One of the eight limbs of Yoga; Its physical postures or seats.

Hecate (Greek) Goddess of the Underworld and the Dark Moon. She was the Goddess of Witchcraft, Magic, and Crossroads.

Hades (Greek) God of the Underworld who represents the unconscious; also called Pluto.

Hephaistos (Greek) The Divine but crippled artisan and blacksmith; Aphrodite's' husband; also called Vulcan.

Hera (Greek) The Queen of the Heavens, and wife of Zeus; also called Juno.

Hermes (Greek) God of Merchants, Thieves, and Travelers. Also represents Thoth Hermes, Egyptian god of wisdom.

Hero "Coming into our own"; used for both men and women.

Hero's Journey Quest for self-identity and unity; a psychological process for achieving balance and integration of the personality.

Hestia (Greek) Virgin Goddess of the Hearth; also called Vesta.

Hetaera (Greek) Divine harlot or temple courtesan.

High Priestess of the Tarot Represents the universal principles of intuitive knowing, inner resourcefulness, and independence.

Holy Ghost Female aspect of the Holy Trinity. See Shekinah.

Horus Egyptian Sun god who was the son of Isis and Osiris.

Hungry Ghosts Buddhist term for souls who were not able to cross the Great Abyss. Cut off from their source of spiritual energy, they wander in the twilight between life and death in a futile effort to complete themselves.

Hydra (Mythological) Seven-headed monster that guarded the golden fleece in the Jason myth.

Individuation (Jungian) Term for integrating the conscious mind with the unconscious in a process which produces a single amalgamation of the whole.

Initiation Stages in life or rites of passage where deep transformational forces are working inside. Also, dramatic rituals performed by secret societies. The laying on of hands by an initiated teacher completes a link that goes back to the dawn of time--like a long term relay race.

Inner Child The little person inside who is the key to our emotional satisfaction and the state of wonderment.

Inner Mother Unconditional loving, nurturing support within.

Inner Sanctuary The peaceful center that is safe from the excitement of the vortex; the temple within.

Integration Synonymous with wholeness, the bringing together of the many god/ess within to form a peaceful unity.

Ishta Devata (Sanskrit) "The God I worship;" one's chosen ideal. It is said that the devotee receives a continuous stream of nectar from the Ishta.

Isis (Egyptian) Moon Goddess who possessed great powers of magic, sorcery, and fertility.

Jason (Greek) Hero whose adventures retrieved the Golden Fleece.

Jonah Biblical being who spent time in the belly of the whale.

Juno (Roman) See Hera.

Jupiter (Roman) King of the Olympian gods and heaven; also called Zeus.

Kali (Sanskrit) Great Mother who has a wrathful side; represents both creation and destruction.

Kali Yuga The age of Kali or the Great Mother.

Kamakaula (Sanskrit) Goddess of the Tantra. See Kaulacharya.

Karma (Sanskrit) Buddhist/Hindu concept of eternal retribution which is best represented by Newton's law of inertia/momentum: "A body in motion tends to remain in motion at the speed and in the direction in which it is traveling."

Kaulacharya (Sanskrit) Term for path of the sexual Tantra, also known as the Red Tantra.

Kundalini The essential sexual force within the body said to reside resting at the base of the spine.

Liberation The freedom one receives as a result of enlightenment. To be freed from the necessity of continual rebirth.

Lila (Sanskrit) Divine sport. The game Gods' play within their own creation.

Litany Verses or small songs recited to evoke Bhakti in the heart of the devotee. See Mantra.

Madonna/Whore Psychological term for the outmoded mindset used to classify women.

Magic Veil See Glamour and Maya.

Mantra (Sanskrit) Holy names or seeds of power. The most powerful are given by spiritual teachers but only under an oath of secrecy where they must be "awakened" through diligent repetition and single-minded attention.

Major Arcana The 22 universal principles or pathways of the tarot.

Mars (Roman) God of War and Aggression; also Ares; our male aspect of the personality that asserts toward desires.

Maya (Sanskrit) The Grand Illusion of life.

Mercury (Roman) See Hermes.

Midwife Archetype that helps birth new life.

Mindset The sum total of all contents of the mind at a given point in time. Includes thoughts, beliefs, and observations.

Metaphysical Meta means beyond, therefore it is the science which lies beyond the physical.

Moon Inner Goddess Powers; feminine and unconscious parts of the personality; can be seen as child, maiden, mother, or crone.

Moon Palace A space where we live by reflected light, the light of others, not our own.

Mudra A hand or body position that rechannels energy.

Nataraja (Hindu) God of Creation who is paired with Sivakama.

Nemesis (Greek) Word for the pent-up energy of the god/ess, which can explode if not properly honored.

Neuro-Linguistic Programming The psychology of understanding and controlling behavior in yourself or others.

Nirvana (Sanskrit) God realization, Satori, cosmic or God consciousness.

Ojas (Sanskrit) The magical essence which results when sexual energy is raised and transmuted in the brain. Purified lust is said to be the fuel of the Higher Self.

Olympus Famous mountain of the Greek god/ess.

Om or Aum The most sacred word, thought to be formed by the sum of all vibrations--the sound of all movement within the universe. See Mantra.

Osiris (Egyptian) God of Death and Rebirth, brother and husband of Isis, father of Horus, the Sun God.

Ouranos (Greek) Sky God who mated with Gaia to form the original Olympian family; also Uranus.

Pearl of Great Price (Biblical) Term for God realization.

Personal Myth The sum of all personal experiences, desires, and dreams that form the personality.

Persephone (Greek and Roman) Archetypal maiden, daughter of Demeter and wife of Hades; represents the principles of self-esteem.

Philosopher's Stone Alchemical reference to God realization.

Pluto (Roman) See Hades.

Projection Psychological term for putting onto others observations and judgments that rightfully belong within ourselves.

Psyche (Greek) A term for the soul; also the goddess who represents our conscious journey to inner completion.

Psychosynthesis A branch of transpersonal psychology.

Qabalah Western occult system of God-realization.

Quan Yin Chinese Goddess of Mercy.

Quest A mystical journey that leads to integration of the soul.

Ragnel Cursed wife of Gawain; our witch-like consciousness that knows how to ask for what we want, and which transforms when we are given our own way.

Ramakrishna Nineteenth-century Hindu monk believed to be a totally enlightened avatar or direct incarnation of God.

Reverie The natural resting state of an average mind that jumps, races, and skips about in nonsensical and irrelevant thought patterns.

Sacred Psychology A spiritual search for identity and unity. See Soulmaking, Quest, the Great Adventure, the Great Work.

Sanskrit Ancient sacred language of the Hindus which has fifty-two phonemes (basic unit of speech), each of which is said to have great power when understood.

Satchidananda (Sanskrit) Sat/existence, Chid/knowledge, Ananda/ bliss; a term use to describe God; also the name of an Eastern guru.

Saturn (Roman) See Cronus.

Scarlet Woman Western occult symbol of a woman who practices the Red Tantra; one who is gifted in the arts of erotic lovemaking. Her role is to entice and excite the male. See Kaulacharya.

Selene Greek Goddess who personified the Moon itself.

Shadow (Psychological) Term for the unknown and often unintegrated parts of ourselves.

Shakti (Sanskrit) Hindu Goddess who embodies the active creative principle. Also Great Mother or Maha Shakti.

Shekinah (Qabalistic) The wondrous Feminine force. See Shakti, Holy Ghost.

Shamanism Primitive spiritual practices that connected man with the forces of nature and the spirits of animals and ancestors.

Siva (Hindu) God of Infinite Potential; also the destroyer of worlds.

Sivakama (Sanskrit) See Kamakaula.

Sorceress Female who has the powers of magic.

Soulmaking The spiritual quest or the development of the soul. See Quest.

Styx (Mythological) River that connects the underworld with the outer life.

Subpersonalities (Psychological) Term for the many faces of the psyche. They are the god/ess within.

Synchronicity (Jungian) Meaningful coincidences; shows how the inner reality fits symbolically with the outer.

Tantra (Sanskrit) Practice leading to enlightenment through conservation and control of sexual energy. (Red Tantra is the sexual or outer practices and the Yellow Tantra is the asexual or inner practices.)

Tantrika (Sanskrit) One who practices the Tantra.

Tao (Chinese) A harmonious way of life; the path of nonattachment and surrender to the flow of the universe.

Tarot Arcane collection of mystical symbols. An ancient book whose pages are not bound. Together with the Qabalah, Tarot forms a complete western method of God realization.

Temple Virgin (Mythological) A sacred prostitute who restores men's connection with their Godself through lovemaking. See Hetaera.

Temptress (Archetypical) The dark side of Aphrodite, who seduces with indulgences.

Theurgy The art of assuming a God-form, becoming a living God or Goddess.

Tiresias (Greek) Mythological man who lived part of his life as a woman. Hera struck him blind, but Zeus offset the blindness with the gift of prophecy.

Tree of Life See Qabalah.

Umbilical Connections Emotional bonds from the past, which are much like a child's need for its mother.

Uranus (Roman) See Ouranos.

Venus (Roman) See Aphrodite.

Vesta (Roman) See Hestia.

Virago (Latin) Female warrior or hero.

Vira (Sanskrit) The hero's attitude.

Virgin (Mythological) Term that means "one unto herself."

Viriditas (German) Greening power; the lush creativity of the regenerative force.

Visionary Quest The search for self-identity and unity; another name for Hero's Journey.

Voluptia (Greek) Psyche and Eros' daughter; her name means plunging into life; also called Pleasure or Joy.

Vortex of Being Metaphor for the whirling mind stuff of consciousness.

Vulcan (Roman) See Hephaistos.

Warrior One who is on the spiritual path and has decided to do battle with the forces of ignorance and injustice within.

Watcher The objective subpersonality that stays conscious and awake throughout every action.

Witch Consciousness Anytime we feel sick, old, or ugly; the part within who knows how to ask for what we want.

Womanly Wonders The boons of the Goddess; another term for beauty, creativity, and sexual magnetism.

Yantra (Sanskrit) Visual mantras of yoga that serve as centering devices and symbolic compositions of the energy patterns of certain forces and deities.

Yoga (Sanskrit) Union, which includes eight limbs: the first two, yama and niyama, teach ethical perfection; the next two, hatha and pranayama, convey the physical postures and breathing exercises; and the last four branches, pratyahara, dharana, dhyana, and samadhi are meditation techniques and states of consciousness.

Yogi One who practices the disciplines of yoga.

Yoga Sutras Ancient distillation of the science of yoga written by Patanjali (c. 300 b.c.). Sutras must be memorized in order for their full power to manifest.

Yoni (Sanskrit) The vagina.

Zen A branch of Buddhism noted for its austere meditation practices and lifestyle.

Zeus (Greek) See Jupiter.

Index

About the Authors

Karen LaPuma is a motivational and spiritual counselor who has been practicing in Northern California since 1979. Karen holds a degree from Penn State where she majored in human potential. In the Bay Area, she is a well known personality who regularly lectures and holds seminars, as well as making occasional appearances on television and radio. Karen has trained extensively in psychology, self-growth techniques, eastern and western mythology, metaphysics, and comparative religions. She wrote a regular astrological advice column for the Marin Independent Journal, founded and edited a monthly newsletter titled "Self Growth," and produced local theatrical productions. *Awakening Female Power* is the result of her research, case histories and personal experiences.

Walt Runkis is an unconventional scientist who is also an initiate of both Eastern and Western schools of metaphysics. He is the inventor of the artificial root system, a complete plant nutrient broth and is the author of dBiz(tm) Accounting System software. The program guide for the San Francisco Celebration of Innovation called him, "a true Renaissance Man: Walt is an inventor, chemist, musician, computer programmer, audio-visual artist, producer, director, sculptor, yogi and metaphysician.

Are You Truly Ready To Find Your Goddess Powers?

Karen LaPuma has teamed up with Steven Halpern to create a companion audio cassette, entitled *Finding the Goddess Within*. Now you can relax in the comfort of your own home as Karen's melodic voice and the musical genius of Steven Halpern reveal how to effortlessly awaken your female power, unlock your divine potential, and transform your life into a joyous dance of fulfillment.

It's like having a personal session, only better. For the past twelve years Karen has been helping people find their God-given purpose by taking them within themselves to see their inate resources. On side one, Karen tells how everyone can transform their daily lives into the adventure of the Hero's Quest. This provides a "theoretical basis" for discovery, and prepares you for the actual inner experience of awakening. On side two, Karen is accompanied by the New Age Sound of Steven Halpern. Together, they create a beautiful guided meditation that will take you deep inside the mansion of your wonderous being. This mystical musical experience is the perfect companion to *Awakening Female Power* because it provides the "hands-on" experience. Reading satifies the mind, but it takes experience to satisfy the soul.

Finding the Goddess Within is a rich and rewarding adventure you won't want to miss. It's a joy that you can experience by yourself or give to those you love and want to empower. If your favorite bookseller does not have *Finding the Goddess Within*, you can get it direct from the publisher by filling out the order form on the next page, or by writing to: *SoulSource Publishing,*

P.O. Box 877,
Fairfax, CA, 94930

Order Form

You're right, I am ready to awaken my female power and empower the Goddess I am inside. I cannot find the Goddess Power I need in my area and want to buy direct from the publisher. Please send me the items I have indicated below or just a free newsletter. I am also happy to hear that *SoulSource Publishing* will pay the freight to my door or will send gift units freight prepaid to my loved ones (California residents must however sent 6.25% sales tax--$.62 for the tape and $.80 for the book).

audio tape: Total

_____Finding the Goddess Within $9.98 ea. . ._____

book:

_____Awakening Female Power $12.95 ea. . . ._____

❑ Free Subscription to Newsletter . . . . __N/C__

❑ California State Sales Tax (6.25%). . . . . ._____

❑ Total Cost. . . . .

❑ Enclosed is my payment for the "Total Cost: above.

❑ Please bill my ❑ MasterCard or ❑ Visa.

_____   _____

Credit Card Number   Exp. Date

_____

Signature

Send this Order or your Name and Address for a **free** subscription to our newsletter, *SoulSource Resource* .

_____

Name

_____

Address

_____

City, State, Zip Code

Mail to: ***SoulSource Publishing***
                        P.O. Box 877
                        Fairfax, CA, 94930